Remember Me

The Life

of a

Walsall Lad

Paul Reeves

First Published in the UK in 2021

ISBN: 9798516765223
Imprint: Independently published

Paul Reeves
Burntwood
Staffordshire

Autumn wind blows
Old leaves from the tree
Winter kills life
From all memory

Spring breathes growth
To branch, twig and leaf
Summer brings fruit
To roots relief

Autumn wind blows
Vita Vadit In

PR©

Contents

Prologue

'A tale of unfathomable scientific connection made between a Victorian policeman and his unsuspecting blood relative almost 100 years after his death. A tale, brought to life beyond the grave when Henry discovers a way to tell his incredible life story through his kinsman Paul. Two timelines become diffracted as Henry embarks on a mission to be remembered. Little does Paul know, they have more in common than he thinks.'

Emily Katherine Paula, (daughter of the author).

Chapter One

Painting a Picture

This testament is the story of my life, based on real experiences between my birth in 1843 and my death in 1923. My entire life unfolded as a drama, filled with memories and moments from the beginning, all the way to the very end. My recollections, will recall and retell my early Victorian days, right the way through to the first quarter of the twentieth century. These are times long gone by, a different world, but a world that shaped the future in which my family now live. It is my hope that this narrative does not read like a documentary of events, it's my story, told my way, for the reader to believe as much or as little as they like. This story is like no other, factual yes, but mysterious also, one I hope will make you reflect and debate the origin of the family. Seen through my eyes and told by my mouth to the ears of my chosen confidant and biographer. With that sentiment in mind, let me tell you about myself.

My name in life was Henry Reeves, an ordinary, everyday, normal kind of bloke, born in the town of Walsall, Staffordshire. Almost one hundred years after my death, I have been gifted an extraordinary chance to tell the world about myself. This really is an incredible opportunity for me, because my life ran out of time, before I really got chance to talk about my adventures. The moral is quite simple, don't leave things too late in life. If you plan to do something, do it, do it now, before your time comes to an abrupt or untimely end. Time belongs to no man and nobody knows this better than me. This story is firstly for my family and secondly for anyone else interested in all those who came before. Life is a blessing, so soak it up and live it well. It really is most precious, probably more precious than you realise at the time. So back to the story.

I was born in Walsall in the county of Staffordshire on the 3rd July 1843, just another Monday in the middle of summer, but the start of my fantastic adventure. [1] The town of Walsall now sits in the new county of West Midlands, but I'm fairly sure the place has not moved since I was born. The poppycock changes to the boundaries make a mockery of the past, as the old county names stood strong for hundreds of years and served us all well. So for all those who ask, I was born in Staffordshire and proud of it.

My birth in 1843 may seem a long time ago, it was the same year the great engineer, Isambard Kingdom Brunel launched the SS Great Britain at Bristol and Charles Dickens published, 'A Christmas Carol'. A captivating book about ghosts from the past, present and future, coming to remind Scrooge what was most important in life. This may become more relevant later or may be just another spooky coincidence.

Let me take you back to those times, by giving you a little flavour of how things used to be when I was born. Walsall was an old medieval market town in the Staffordshire countryside, situated between the town of Wolverhampton and the city of Lichfield. It sounds quite quaint when you say it like that, but Walsall was fast becoming a player in the industrial heartlands of the Midlands. The whole area was beginning to earn itself a new name, the Black Country, mainly consisting of the boroughs of Walsall, Dudley, Sandwell and parts of Wolverhampton. This area became the engine house of the nation and its natives were a proud bunch of gritty grafters full to the brink with character. The name itself derives most likely from the blackness bellowed out from the fires of industry, burning the rich black seams of coal dug from below the ground on which it sits. It was very black at its industrial high, it was sooty, grimy and people tended to speak as they found, so that's how the name was born. That's my understanding of the Black Country name and I'm sticking to it. Some may dispute this, either through snobbery or through ignorance. Some nincompoops deliberate, debate and then disagree about what the Black Country is, but I was there. Some want to stake their claim to it and some want to distance themselves from the name, its personal choice. Back in 1843 the industrial revolution was rapidly changing the face of the world forever and it spread like wildfire from town to town. Walsall had already begun to draw in hundreds of extra people to lift the heavy hammers needed for this new age. Cheap labour was being sucked in from other villages and even countries, resulting in a steady flow of migrants looking to make their fortune. It is fair to say, not all these people were local or even English. It was the towns first real taste of cosmopolitanism.

Modern day Walsall is almost unrecognisable to the one I knew. The main blame rests with twentieth century planners for demolishing a lot of very good looking historic buildings. When clearing the slums in the 1920s and 30s, they must have been blind. Architecturally they threw the baby out with the bath water!

The nineteenth century town of Walsall was a busy hive of industry and enterprise, all taking place within the sight of the almost timeless St. Matthew's church. High above the High Street, its majestic spire stands like an old friend and beacon, working like a sundial to cast its shadow over the commanding hilltop position. Originally, the church was at the centre of the town with a network of narrow streets spanning out like the roots of a tree and spreading down the hill. There was a labyrinth of Georgian courtyards tucked away and secreted through shadowy alley ways. These slum back-to-backs were crammed full of smelly hovels that people called home. I will never forget those damp and dingy crowded rooms we lived in. Where we gathered together to eat and sleep, struggling to survive the dark clouds of poverty. Some families had to cohabit with their animals, such as pigs and the like, they were terribly squalid and unsanitary places. Animals were not kept

5

as pets back then they were fed for food, there was no emotional attachment to something that filled your stomach. Men, women and children eked out an existence in small dim lit workshops, where they laboured for hours from dusk till dawn just to eat. Outside the sound of horses hooves echoed from the walls as they dragged the laden iron wheeled carts behind. The cobbles were often covered in a minefield of oss muck, drenched with urine. Just one of the hazards that had to be avoided on a daily basis. I know those early times sent a very real escape message to my brain, that I never forgot with the passing of years.

On market day, stalls unfolded and cascaded down the hill of the High Street, from the church all the way down to the bridge at the bottom. A multitude of traders congregated to sell their goods. They competitively screamed out their latest bargains to the scurrying local people who came to shop. In those times the market went on all day, as late as ten o'clock at night. Eventually the town constable rang the bell, instructing them to pack up for the day and go home. That bell had a very clear sound and message that always reverberated in my mind. It was much later that I realised why that sound meant so much. Walsall was once a major hog market with all the squealing, snorting and other nasties that went with it. Like the pigs of the past, my story has a few squeals and a good twist in the tail.

So to live with the pungent wafting aroma of muck, sweat and toil meant you had to be resilient and a fully paid up member of the community team. Everybody relied on everybody else, just to get through to the next day. Perhaps you think I am painting a bleak picture, but that's the way it was.

Walsall was already renown for its leather goods back in the 1840s. We kept the horse drawn world rolling, producing everything from saddles, bridles, harnesses, collars and whips. Equine wares from the town supplied the whole British Empire and beyond. Almost every

6

trade and profession, was peppered within the towns ancient boundaries. Metal trades supplemented the leather works by making horse brassware, buckles, spurs, stirrups and bits. There really was a tremendous skill base of local experienced and accomplished craftsmen and women. Despite the canals and trains getting closer, it was still the time of the horse and would be for several decades to come. Most of the time, fumes from the forges, curriers, tanners and abattoirs stunk the place out. Our only sanctuary was the more pleasant bakers and brewers when we passed by their way. Smells of all kinds floated from street to street, like the perfume and fragrance of life. I have to say the majority of them were not good.

Tanners needed to use human urine to help the leather tanning process. Hides were soaked in the amber fluid to assist with removing the hair from the skin. Supposedly, poor people saved their urine and took it to the tanners for a small reward, getting the name, 'Piss Poor'. The even more impoverished didn't have 'A Pot to Piss In'. I think you are getting the picture of Walsall at the time. Not everyone was poor, there were rich people as well. The two were entirely different, incompatible by breed and rarely did their worlds collide, except for when one served the other.

Every street and alleyway was endowed and interspersed with inns, taverns and alehouses. These were magnets for local people to come together and discuss the days tribulations. The tête-à-tête gossiping slowly softened the drudge of their day with the medication of the in-house brew. It wasn't always a case of softening the drudge, sometimes the grog was used as dope to leave the world altogether. Throughout time man has always tried to find a way to deaden the feelings of a struggling mind. At this time in history it was ale. To survive you had to work, so too much beer would lead to disaster and doom. I should point out, some of my terminology may be old fashioned, even offensive. You have to remember, I came from a very different time

7

over a century and a half ago. Times were very different back then, so don't judge too harshly and please don't use present day standards as a benchmark. It's like hammering a square peg into a round hole, it just won't go, things were not even remotely similar back then. I doubt that many people can empathise without having experienced the upbringing handed to me. In any case, I'm not looking for sympathy.

When I grew up there was immeasurable social injustice. We didn't have the luxury of being offended or being able to demand an apology. Every decent working class person in Victorian England was shackled to their class and exploited by their bosses. People had no choice but to toe the line, or crash and burn. The world of the working classes was far from hospitable or predictable. For the majority, life expectancy was short. Nobody turned a head at the sight of a baby coffin box passing through the poor house streets. A tip of the cap and a passing thought was all the poor souls got, if they were lucky. Death was so matter of fact.

To paint you a picture, our central heating, was a coal fire, when we could afford to light it. Not to say that we only burnt coal, we torched whatever we could get our hands on to keep warm. With the bonus of a bit of flickering light, the flames were our only source of heat and our means of cooking. The privy was quite rightly stuck outside the back of the house and shared with all the neighbours. It was freezing cold in the winter and stinking rancid in the summer. I can tell you, nobody wanted to queue with our neighbours for the toilet or share their personal aroma! At night a guzunda came to the fore, a long gone necessity to save you the walk across the dark icy cold yard. The whole family knew when the guzunda was in use, the rule was no number two's. All our water came from a standpipe in the courtyard, God knows how clean that water was. It tasted awful at times, not even fit to wash your stinking socks. Mother boiled the drinking water, but I was still not convinced, it was safe. There were few things to make our days easy and little or no money to buy them anyway.

News and gossip came locally by word of mouth, most people were uneducated, illiterate and unable to read the newspapers. Sadly people could not even write their own name, which tethered them to a life of physical labour and drudge. An 'X' was the only mark they could manage to make on official documents, such as marriage and birth certificates. Knowledge was power and the rich and privileged strived to keep it for themselves. Money made money and the rich wanted to keep it from the workers for themselves. Paying good wages was bad for business, but times were changing. I had a feeling that our generation was going to make a difference.

Medicines were few and far between and failed to prevent everyday disease. Cholera, typhoid and smallpox cut them down like the grim reaper's scythe. In just one epidemic, the young, the old and the infirm could be swept away. A deathly shadow of disease was often cast over the whole community.

There were no antibiotics, the strong survived and the rest died, it was as simple as that. Penicillin wasn't even discovered until 1928 and that was still a lifetime away. Public hygiene was a contradiction in terms, mortality and the passing of life was matter of fact. There was no health service to save you when sickness developed. A typical family was a large one, although the prospect of a child reaching the age of five was far from guaranteed. In fact it was more of an achievement with the odds being against it. In an environment that suppressed life from flourishing, nothing was a certainty. Women spent most of their fertile years in a pregnant condition with death being a real possibility at every birth. Infant and mother deaths were a major factor in controlling the population. Family planning was still very much a thing for the future. Nevertheless, women had to bring up their brood and look after their men irrespective of what life threw their way. People made their bed and had no choice but to lie in it. It was not the time of opportunity, people were held down. One bad decision could have a whole short lifetime of consequences to deal with. In these times of hand to mouth survival, workdays were long, pay was poor and working conditions, dangerous and demanding. The working classes were the expendable commodity upon which the Empire was built and relied upon. Life really was cheap, to the rich we were but their beasts of burden. If you became incapable of working, your unconcerned employer would give you a farewell, there was no offer of welfare. There was no contract of employment to fall back on, no sickness leave and certainly no redundancy, paternity or maternity benefits. You were on your own, reliant on your ability to survive, with family and friends as your only back-up and safety net. Men died every day at work from accidents, shear neglect, lack of safety or just outright exhaustion. It was just pot luck if you made it through to the next day. You have heard the term, living wage, well in those days, if you didn't earn you didn't live.

Circumstance forced people to evolve into resourceful creatures, forging a pathway in life through brute strength and determination. My people were resolute, resilient and had an unbreakable determination to get to the next day. The ones without those special qualities fell by the wayside in the cruel world of natural selection. The church offered us spiritual salvation, but everyday life dictated what we did to survive. Family came first and the rights and wrongs second. Despite the bleakness, we managed to make ends meet by making or taking what we needed. When the poor found themselves 'Up before the beak' on the wrong side of the law, the courts delivered harsh punishments. I'm sure the rich magistrates sometimes based the fines on what they personally could afford. There was always the alternative of prison for those who could not or would not pay. There was no legal aid and the authorities made examples of those who transgressed, it was their job to send out a clear message to deter others.

It is a wonder those dirty working class people even managed to get a generation through to the future. We started as ragamuffin kids dressed in substandard filthy hand-me-downs, but somehow we made it through to give our children brighter times.

That was the reality of life, let me now talk about my own origins and family background leading up to 1843 and the start of my life.

Chapter Two

Setting the Scene

S kipping back another couple of generations takes us to a little picturesque elevated Staffordshire village, called Chapel Chorlton. The year was 1820 and although the Industrial Revolution had begun, it certainly had not come to this little place. As the church bell rang out on the last Sunday of February 1820, my grandmother Margaret Higginson walked to the door of St. Lawrence's church. [2] She was carrying her young baby daughter Margaret Cinderella, my mother to be baptised wrapped in a warm blanket. Her middle name really was Cinderella, meaning 'a little girl from the ashes'. This was romanticised through the pantomime story, a hope to rise from 'Rags to Riches'. My grandmother was christened in the same church less than nineteen years previous in the presence of her parents, Thomas and Ann. [3] Grandmother Margaret was a popular and well-known member of the congregation of St. Lawrence's. On that day she felt alone. Tongue's wagged as she walked down the aisle taking a seat near the front. She was after all an unmarried woman who had conceived my mother out of wedlock. This was a terrible stigma at the time, heavens knows why, we are all supposed to be God's children. She wasn't the first to be in this position and would not be the last. It was little conciliation and did not make the finger pointing any easier to stomach. The father was conspicuous by his absence, he being the chemist Michael Hall or so thats what her marriage certificate says. [4] For whatever reason, be it failure or refusal he had not done the decent thing and had left Margaret to the challenges of motherhood alone. I would just like to say at this point that there are some very strong women in this story and she is one of them. Times were very judgemental and cruel with words like bastard and base being used. All because the kids father was not married to the mother. In my opinion, the women in my world were all equal to the men and often proved stronger. Despite their individual strengths and intelligence, they seldom got the credit or status except from the family they built.

Grandmother Margaret was alone on that day, but she had hope and vision to light her way. Just two years later in July 1822, she married Thomas Halfpenny in the neighbouring parish of Seighford. Margaret my mother was brought up with several other children that followed. Some of those children survived and some perished as victims of the time. [5] Grandmother Margaret lived into her late eighties and died at the end of January in 1890. [6] Thomas had died early 1873 leaving her a widow for the last seventeen years of her life. [7] Mother often spoke about her mother but I can't remember her being a part of our lives.

This story continues with my mother Margaret Cinderella, who was to become the matriarch and foundation stone to get the family through the next fifty years. Every good son looks up to their mother and despite her failings she did her best in the face of environmental and social adversity. She was such a hero to me and woe betide anyone who said any different in my presence. She was soft and gentle to the ones she loved, but could defend her family like a gladiator to the death if required.

The fact my mother and father met at all, can all be blamed on an Act of Parliament passed in 1833. This granted approval to begin construction on the Grand Junction Railway designed by George Stephenson and Joseph Locke, two of the Victorian Age's most notorious engineers. This Act lit the fuse that allowed the Industrial Revolution to blast its way through the green fields of Staffordshire, passing close to the small village where Margaret lived. Huge armies of workmen descended on the unspoilt rural villages and towns, completely changing them forever. A young skilled bricklayer named

Thomas Reeves was one of this marching army of workmen. His skills were in great demand in the building frenzy that saw the line completed in just a few years. In 1836, Thomas caught the eye of my sixteen year old mother, Margaret. He was confident, strong in physique with a curiously coarser accent than hers. This was despite originating from only a few miles away near Tipton. Romance flourished and although still relatively a child, life's harshness of upbringing had prepared mother well for the future. It was time for her to find her own 'greener grass', away from the village. This was still at a time when a boy could marry at fourteen and a girl at twelve with consent. This only highlights how times really were different back then, childhood was such a different concept. It wasn't until the Marriage Act of 1929 that the age was raised to sixteen, but that was still almost one hundred years away. Life expectancy was so much less at the time, so people just had to crack on I suppose. Mother was literally swept off her feet by Thomas. The great industrial age was coming into full bloom, promising a bright and enlightened future. The winter of 1836 was bitterly cold and as Christmas approached the couple went to Tipton, a village deep in the dark region that Thomas originated from. It was there in St. Martin's church in mid-December 1836 that Margaret Cinderella Higginson married Thomas Reeves. [8] The witnesses to the wedding ceremony were local prominent members of the church congregation, one being the local registrar. Within only a few short months of the wedding my mother found herself in a family predicament. She was expecting their first child and with my father at her side, it was exciting times.

My dad was laying bricks in Birmingham when their first child William arrived just before Christmas 1837. [9] The freezing bleak end to that year saw a full covering of winter snow. Mum often spoke about the time William being born being cold. Dad's skills as a bricklayer promised him work on the great railway lines, which were spreading like a spiders web all across the country. He was a journeyman bricklayer, who moved progressively along the course of the tracks, building cuttings, tunnels, embankments, station platforms and bridges. These railway lines left deep lasting scars on the countryside, but this was progress, the way forward. The reality was, my mother was left alone most of the time to manage the day-to-day tasks single handed. She was tough, but then again she had to be. My sister Sarah, was born two years later at Burton-upon-Trent in 1839, near the route of the Birmingham and Derby Junction Railway. [10] This was the work of Robert Stephenson, George's son and it opened later that year.

By 1841, my mother was lodging in Lawley Street, Birmingham with her two children while dad was working away. [11] This part of town contained the terminus of the Birmingham and Derby Junction Railway. It was not a salubrious place to reside, notoriously rough, a place with gangs and villains roaming the streets causing terror and intimidation. Later the family moved to Wainwright Street, Aston where they had another son Thomas Edward. [12] Sadly the little fellow perished at just fifteen months old and he was buried at Aston churchyard. [13] [14] Birmingham wasn't the second city at this time, that didn't come for another forty-eight years when Queen Victoria upgraded the place in 1889. I guess dad's buildings helped make it all happen or that is what I like to think. Dad's work slowly drew the family towards the town of Walsall, with the railway lines clawing their way towards Bescot. Mother moved there with the children just before I was born in July 1843. I was baptised at St. Mary's the Mount in November 1843 with my brother William. [15] To this day, I'm not certain what was going on with mothers spiritual thoughts. This was a Catholic church but it probably had membership benefits. She was always forward thinking, life was a game of chess and she liked to get her family in the strongest position possible. She had already lost one child and was about to sadly lose another. My brother Peter was born in September 1845, but sadly also died just four months later. [16] [17] I can't remember that much about

15

my dad, he was always at work and most of the time living away from home. In 1847 the South Staffordshire Railway connected the old Grand Junction Railway station at Bescot to Walsall town centre. Initially to Bridgeman Place and then from April 1849 to the new Jacobean style station at Station Street. The old station building which is still there, meant Walsall town centre was finally connected to the rest of the world by iron tracks. Birmingham was now just a short train ride away and somehow the world began to seemingly shrink as new things and places came within easy reach of the population. People began to know so much more, even me I'm pleased to say. Mother got me some lessons at Sunday school and I soon picked up how to read and write. I was now considered a scholar and educated, a step in the right direction, mothers vision was working out. She always told me that knowledge was power and power opened doors, she was such a clever woman. I remember her asking me to write her name, she was fascinated by the letters I wrote on the paper. Another brother George, who was born in the spring of 1847, died in 1849 aged two. [18] [19] I remember crying when he passed, it was my first real recollection of death. I vividly remember his little white body being in the house until he was taken to be buried. That cold vision haunted my dreams for many years during my childhood. Looking back my mother was so brave, she was seven months pregnant with my brother Enoch, when George died in July. He was the third son she had lost, within only a few short years. Enoch my favourite brother arrived in September 1849. He always looked up to me as a kid, we got on so well and were very close. [20]

The population of Walsall was rapidly increasing, rising from 20,852 in 1841 to 26,816 in 1851. This growing population was being squeezed into the old and already overcrowded poor housing. As numbers went up living conditions suffered.

At the end of March 1851, my mother Margaret was effectively the head of the family. We resided in a courtyard type house in Ablewell

16

Street, Walsall, a house already old, dilapidated and shoddily built to begin with. [21] Let's just say that building regulations were not regulated at that time. I'm telling you that some of those places were lucky to still be standing. Mother was working as a laundress taking in washing to supplement dads pay and we also had a couple from Ireland lodging with us to make ends meet. The lodgers, Micky Melbourne and his wife Liz could swear and drink like there was no tomorrow. Times were terribly hard for mother and she was pregnant again with another brother, Abel who was born in September 1851. My elder brother William who was only thirteen was working as a labourer. My sister Sarah at just eleven was the live in servant of Tom Hathaway a blacksmith from Caldmore. [22] Dad was away from home lodging in Burslem, employed on the new North Staffordshire Railway.

Just when I thought nothing could get worse, it did. I remember walking into the house and mum was crying inconsolably with the young ones doing the same in ignorant unison. Nobody spoke a word, so I knew it must be bad. Eventually mum told me, dad was dead, he was only forty-one for Gods sake. He had no right to leave us in this world of pain. I was mad and sad all at the same time, how could this happen? The world taught me in a cruel and brutal fashion that everyone travelling this road of life has to get off at some time. It happened to be his turn on that fateful day. When I think about all those countless bricks dad laid though out his short life. All at the expense of his family time, it deeply grieves me. I suppose he did what he had to do, but that does not make it any easier to bare. His reward for a life's enterprise of building railways, was a pittance of pay and a legacy of tracks. Some of which Dr. Beeching's axe swept away just a hundred years later in the 1960s.

Mum had been left up the creek without a paddle with a family to provide for and no husband to support her. It was almost impossible for a widowed working class woman to survive on her own. There was certainly no equal rights or equal pay. The working class were the lowest of the low and their women even lower.

What really happened to dad was a mystery, his death was never spoken about after that day.

Benjamin Hammond was a friend and acquaintance of my dad, another bricklayer by trade. He was two years younger than mum and a country boy, having been born in a rural place called Ludlow in Shropshire. He had followed his own father as a bricklayer into the lucrative building boom and like mum had ended up in Walsall. Mums options were not great but her loyalty was to her children. With that in mind she and Benjamin were married at St. Peter and St. Paul's church, Aston in November 1853. [23] This was the first of many family weddings at Aston. Although the vicar was told the couple resided in Aston, they actually lived in Walsall. I think it was just to have a day out or it may have been so mother could visit the resting place of my brother Thomas Edward. Thanks to my dad and his fellow workers, Aston was now only a train ride away. I was ten at this time and felt like a fish out of water with a new man around. I didn't want or need another father, but looking back, this wasn't about me, mother needed another husband for the family to make it.

With the new step-father came the inevitable half-brothers. Four in all, first Benjamin in 1854, James in 1856, George in 1859 and finally Edward in 1861. [24] [25] [26] [27] George perished as an infant another casualty of the times at just two years of age. [28] Mum had twelve children in total, a football team of boys and one girl. Four of the boys died before reaching the age of five, that's a third of all her children! The new Hammond boys shared mums genes and were my half-brothers, but Christ we were like chalk and cheese. That was to become blatantly obvious as time went on.

In 1858 my sister Sarah had a son, William who was born at the Union workhouse. [29] The father was a Walsall copper named O'Tool but

18

he never shaped up to the task and abandoned her. My eldest brother William, left home soon after to work on the narrow boats at Birchills. This was the area where the canal network entered Walsall town and was still a substantial carrier of freight. He worked all his life for George Moor on the waterways so I never really saw much of him always working away on the water.

Chapter Three

Flying the Nest

There wasn't a great deal of choice open to me when I got to sixteen in 1859. I just knew working in a dirty and toxic fume filled factory would consign me to an early grave. I only had to think of dad to remind me that life could be cut short. I knew I had to break out of the claustrophobic grimy streets of Walsall, which were as restrictive as prison bars. I didn't want to be in Walsall or prison, there was a big world out there and it was time for me to broaden my horizons. I refused to fall prey to the inevitable lifestyle mapped out by my surroundings and birth. I was determined to spring out of the rat trap and escape the soot and smoke from the chimneys.

On 3rd July 1859 it was my sixteenth birthday. There were ten of us living in that tiny house in Pool Street, Chuckery. Mother was also pregnant with another baby due in the autumn. I was a fair size for my age and I had been talking to a local copper, Police Constable Childs. He told me about his army time in India and about seeing the world. His recommendations and advice was gratefully received and helped me make up my mind. The army was always looking for lads like me.

A fortnight later on the 18th July 1859, I received the Queen's Shilling and took the plunge into the unknown. [30] When I told the family I was going, mum had a tear in her eye. I think it was the fact that all her hard work had come to fruition and she was proud I had managed to escape my lot.

After saying my goodbye's off I went to Aldershot barracks. It was my first experience of long distance rail travel and to be fair, I was impressed. I realised my dad's bricklaying endeavours had actually achieved something worthwhile, something for the greater good. I

20

arrived in Aldershot to discover I was entering a hard world of no nonsense. Victorian military discipline was structured and strict with a lot of shouting and swearing thrown in. Soldiering was not the career for the faint hearted and I was proper rocked to the core by the change. It was a totally different life, the army was my mother now after all. My hard upbringing had prepared me well but I was missing my mothers presence all the same. I was taught the essential ingredients of marching and how to use a musket with a sharp bayonet attached. To be honest the drill was rammed down our throats, but at least I had a smart red uniform to wear. The British army was a scary machine, no wonder our enemies were reluctant to fight us. I was soon aware the boy from Walsall was being knocked out of me and rapidly being replaced by a very different man, shaped by the British Army. My new family was one that would last forever, where ever I went, my brothers would be there. Just to make things clear, I was no longer just the lad from Walsall, I was Private 935 Henry Reeves of the 99th Regiment of Foot, man of the world. I wasn't being paid to think, just to listen and do as I was told. Enlisting with the British military unceremoniously and dramatically plunged me into the next chapter of my life. The military ran like clockwork and to the book. The Victorian Imperial Age was at its height in the 1850s and the Empire covered a third of the globe. The foundation stone of the status and power was the large and powerful army and navy. What the hell had I done, I was about to find out.

The 99th Regiment of Foot wasn't just any old regiment, far from it. I had only joined one of the elite units. The saying, 'Dressed up to the Nines' came from my regiment being the best at drill and turnout in the whole army. That was the story the drill sergeant told us so it must be true. We were expected to keep up an immaculate and impeccable reputation at all times and with no exceptions. At the end of September 1858 my regiment had left England for Berhampore barracks, in West Bengal, India. I knew when training was completed I would be following them there. A few days after passing out from training my name was called out, together with a couple of the other lads destined for the 99th regiment. We had to get all our kit together, we were literally shipping out! Soon we were ready to move out from the barracks for the coast, where there was a waiting troop carrier. Troop transport by ship was not a luxury cruise, it was grim and meant being crammed into a small place with all the other men. It was cramped, dirty and rations were in short supply. Food was preserved for long life for the voyage and was less than scrumptious shall we say.   In fact most of the life and flavour was all but preserved out of it. Discipline was strict, I knew I was the lowest of the low. I only spoke when spoken to and learnt my place in the pecking order. To be fair, it was the only safe way to travel to say as little as possible. Having boarded, I found a corner of the ship to live whilst enduring the voyage. The younger lads were all in the same boat so to speak and tended to stick together. I recall looking back at the English shoreline as we sailed away. I wondered if I was ever going to see my mother or even ever return to my homeland again. I was looking forward to seeing what was in store at India, but apprehensive about the whole thing. I couldn't help but think that things had irreversibly changed forever. The rickety old ship, creaked and cracked, with every wave but I soon managed to find my sea legs. I needed to, we were weeks away from India and living on board ship was something to be reckoned with. The vessel was infested with rodents and insects making it a challenge for us to eat the food before they got it. I never realised as I sailed away from my country that night, it would be over ten long years before I returned.

Unknown to us, our lords and masters were discussing events in the far east while we sailed towards India. The Chinese had breached a trading agreement signed with Britain in 1858 and while we travelled, the generals were making battle plans. Their sabre rattling was leading fast towards a military engagement, meaning I was about to have a baptism of fire. The British government were trying to persuade the Chinese to observe the treaty allowing us to trade opium in China. The Chinese emperor opposed those rights, but the British and French were prepared to reinforce it by force if necessary. This obviously meant the use of the military and that now meant me.

I was one of ninety-two new privates who joined the regiment in Calcutta in January 1860. When I arrived there was already a frenzy of activity and buzz about the place. The regiment had already received its orders, to proceed to Hong Kong in preparation for possible active service. The conflict would come to be known as the Second Opium War. Two companies from the regiment had already left Calcutta and had sailed on board HMS Adventurer. At only sixteen I found myself half-way around the world in India. This was a completely different world to England. Men were loading supplies onto the ships ready for us to depart, in what seemed like an organised and well rehearsed fashion. It did take ages to get anywhere by ship, so there could be no hanging about. The screaming and shouting of orders was deafening, the sergeants could shout for England and probably be heard there from India. When the general whispered his orders at the top, they were always boomed out when they reached us at the bottom. Despite the harshness, there was still a strong camaraderie, a feeling you were part of a big family. The lads could be knocking seven bells out of each other one minute and best of mates the next. During the first week in February 1860, a couple of days after getting to India we set sail. The whole regiment boarded three ships the HMS Walmer Castle, HMS Octavia and HMS Mars. These ships were unbelievably infested with all kinds of crawling bugs, that got everywhere. The worst things were massive flying cockroaches at least one and a half inches in size. I had never seen anything like them back at home! I had escaped from Walsall, but had I jumped out of the frying pan into the fire? I got the feeling I was about to find out the answer.

Lieutenant General Sir James Hope Grant was appointed as the commander of all the British forces involved in the operation. He had already reached Hong Kong and was standing by for news from the diplomats. They had set the deadline date of the 8th April 1860, for the Chinese to comply with the British government's demands. The general had a distinguished military career and had fought in China previously. In preparation he ordered the 99th Regiment to proceed to Chusan (Zhoushan). We were to make up part of a two thousand strong force in readiness of war being declared. The rest of this force was made up from the 67th Regiment, Rotten's Battery of artillery and some engineers.

Needless to say the Chinese did not play ball and in due course the deadline passed and we declared war on China. We all knew this would mean fighting the Chinese on their home soil, which was a massive home advantage. To say I was scared was an under statement, China was full of mystery and we knew their warriors were accomplished swordsmen. China was an ancient land with very mysterious people to the British. It had a long history, they invented gunpowder the firepower of modern warfare. Our senior men in the ranks were not scared of anything, most had seen action in India or Africa and thought that the Chinese had no chance. I just hoped they were right, I suppose they had the experience to know about fighting. Being on board those ships was tedious and mind bending, there was nowhere to escape for a quiet moment. To help with entertainment, the officers allowed the men to stage cock fights on the deck. In the main, most of the men were a rough bunch of blood thirsty types thrilled by booze fuelled gore. Army life was a gateway to cruelty and I had walked straight through it. The reality was the regiment consisted of a gang of trained killers, who for money would kill and euthanise the enemy with the minimum of fuss and emotion. Mentally I was being swung around by the feet, viewing the world through kaleidoscope eyes as I travelled from England to

India and now towards China. In only a few months, time certainly began to weave the threads of adventure into the rich tapestry of my life.

By the end of February we had reached Singapore, but were refused permission to stop. This was a catastrophe for the mental welfare and expectations of the men who were desperate to get off that filthy ship for a while. Unfortunately 1860 was a time long before mental health was a consideration. Instead our orders were to forge on towards the harbour at Hong Kong. It was the third week of March 1860 by the time we got there. The place was rammed with military personnel, naval ships and the like, so much so, they would not let us disembark here either. Instead we had to sit tight on board and wait for instructions. The time we spent in Hong Kong harbour seemed to last an eternity. It dragged and dragged and was much longer than we thought it was going to be. In fact it wasn't until almost three weeks into April that we finally lifted our anchor and sailed for Chusan. This place was going to serve as a base for the whole operation. Chusan had been held by the British between 1840 and 1846 following the First Opium War of 1840.

Three days later we arrived at our destination, the regiment numbered thirty officers and eight hundred and ninety-nine men. At great relief to us all, we eventually disembarked on the 26th April. We went ashore wearing our bright red tunics, white trousers and a Kilmarnock head dress with white linen neck flaps. We all carried distinctive black leather back packs laden with kit. On the back was displayed the number ninety-nine, so everybody knew which regiment we belonged to. Everything in the army revolved around a number, that's just the way it was. I have to admit, we did look good as we marched off the decking to the tempo of the drummers beat. The big wigs all watched from a distance, monitoring the way we performed under pressure.

It was the lull before the storm and the lads were having a good time drinking and playing cards with the occasional fight or two. Some of the men were not the sort you messed with, they were after all, trained assassins with plenty of experience. Despite this, most of the hardest men were more afraid of the sergeants than the enemy. Military discipline was very swift and harsh and all kinds of stories circulated about what had happened to people in the past. Men could receive lashings for disobedience and these were cruel and calculated beatings to teach a lesson. Some of these tales were hard to work out whether they were true or the drunken ramblings of mad men in the regiment. Some of these fighting men were bordering on being lunatics and it was safest to keep your distance just in case. I got the impression that at any minute some might howl at the moon like a wolf, they were that crazy. There was just something about the way they stared but didn't speak that chilled to the bone. Maybe it was something that the army turned men into after a while, something that would happen to me.

On the evening of the 17th May, Major General Sir Robert Napier arrived and took control of the Second Division of which the 99th Regiment formed a part. He was a well respected man with many years of military experience mainly in India. Some years later he was elevated to the highest rank in the army of Field Marshal. When he died in 1887 he received a national hero's state funeral at St. Paul's in London.

The regiment re-boarded the troop carriers, HMS Mars, HMS Imperieuse and HMS Burlington in early June 1860. We were to proceed by sailing to Talienwan Bay. A small force of two-hundred men were left under the command of Captain Burton to garrison and protect Chusan. A week later we arrived at Talienwan Bay anchoring with about twenty other Royal Naval vessels from the fleet. I felt great pride and a sense of belonging being part of the pomp and ceremony of the event. I thought about my family back in England and what they

26

might have made of it all. It was certainly an eye opening experience and one that I was never going to forget. It was a tremendous experience for a young man to have sailed to China at such a time in history, magnificent. The sights were truly amazing and would have been unimaginable to me only a few months earlier. Talienwan Bay is located on the southern peninsula of Liaodong, Manchuria. It measures nine miles, north to south and thirteen miles, east to west. There were a number of small bays suitable for landing areas along its coast. Victoria Bay, Hand Bay and Pearl Bay were all close together on north east side and Odin Bay was only few miles further south.

This operation was a spectacular exhibition of military logistics at its best, a demonstration to the rest of the world of the British military muscle being flexed. In 1860 it was fact, not arrogance, that the British military could conquer the world. Getting all those men, horses, guns and ammunition to the other side of the world was an amazing extraordinary achievement a wonder in fact!

Not long after, at the end of June we shifted position to Odin Bay. There we waited for Lieutenant General Sir Hope Grant's permission on where we could encamp. Two days later we moved to Hand Bay, I'm not sure why, but 'left hand, right hand' comes to mind. It's fair to say, a lot was going on behind the scenes, we weren't privilege to. We were but mere pawns in this massive game of Chinese chess, or that's the way it felt to us.

Our French allies on this campaign were no where near as well organised, in fact they were not even ready. It took until mid-July, another two weeks for them to catch up with our operations. Our lads just wanted to get on with things and many either disliked or mistrusted the French. It had only been forty-five years since the French defeat at the Battle of Waterloo and some of their fathers still spoke about it. We were mortal enemies at Waterloo and that feeling of rivalry had not entirely left the ranks. On the 4th July we were finally granted

27

permission to go ashore and camp up on the hills overlooking the sea. It was a great relief to the lads and each regiment of the division had their own hilltop to command. Sentries were posted on watch at night, with a view of the other hilltops. Lights and campfires could be seen for miles. It was a frightening time and my senses got more apprehensive about what was unfolding as time went by. To be honest the thought of death was with me, but I prayed that I could stay safe and see my family again in times to come. It didn't scare me, I had seen death before, but this kind of death was different, potentially violent and of a premeditated kind. I had to trust my comrades in arms to get me through. They were strangely matter of fact about events, they never seemed fearful in front of the younger lads and that reassured us. I think the years of military experience had just desensitised them by almost surgically removing their emotions. I knew that the men at my side could be relied upon in times of trouble, every last one of them.

Lieutenant General Sir James Hope Grant inspected the division in preparation, on the 18th July. Afterwards the military commanders met to discuss tactics for the invasion of China. We marched back to Odin Bay a few days later, where we started digging defensive earthworks fortifying the place as a supply fort. All provisions were transported by sea and it took two days for the tents to arrive. One of the decisions made was to defend the new supply base at Odin Bay with the 99th Regiment of Foot. We now numbered nineteen officers and five-hundred and seventy-nine men. Staying with us were the 19th Punjabi Infantry, consisting of eight British and ten native officers and four-hundred and fifty-three men, together with one hundred artillerymen with six guns. We were tasked to defend the supplies at Odin and for a moment we all thought we were going to be left at the tail end of things. Some of the men were not happy and that evening vented their disapproval by slagging off the top brass. I genuinely thought we had been spared from the action when the main force left Odin Bay on the

26th July. I watched our impressive fleet of seventy-three British and forty French vessels out at sea, each prepared and equipped for the task in hand. They proudly displayed their colours which waved in the cool sea breeze. Every ship looked ready for the anticipated action to come.

Our stay at the supply base was short lived, when orders unexpectedly arrived that a further two companies were to advance leaving only two behind. We boarded HMS Australian on the 8th August, arriving two days later at Beitang. These were exciting times, with something always going on, there was no chance to catch a quiet moment. At Beitang we went out on small boats and were billeted in filthy houses with very little water. I thought at this point, had my life really advanced from my days in Walsall, I began to wonder! Beitang was just about as miserable as it can get. Rain had already turned the vile stinking place into a muddy cesspit. The smell was atrocious with animal carcasses everywhere, including dead cats and dogs. The relentless rain had driven the natives from the town, leaving their grim houses to us.

British forces under the command of Lieutenant General Sir James Hope Grant numbered eleven thousand. The French commander, General Charles Guillaume Cousin-Montauban, had six-thousand seven-hundred men. Our commanding officer of the 99th Regiment was Lieutenant-Colonel George Marmaduke Reeves. Although not a relative, I was happy for anyone who thought he was, to carry on thinking it. It never hurts to have friends in high places, that's what I always say. The fact was he had risen through the ranks of the 99th Regiment from Captain and had over thirty years experience. We were in good hands, he commanded a great deal of respect from both the rank and file and the top brass. He had earned himself the reputation of a force to be reckoned with.

The main advance began on the 12th August 1860 with nine-thousand, three-hundred and thirty-three British and four-thousand

French troops. As part of the 2nd Division, we found the march a heavy slog, lugging all the kit in the very boggy conditions. None of us could afford the luxury of daydreaming, just in case the enemy suddenly attacked. This was China, the enemies home ground. They knew this place very well and could use the terrain to their own advantage. We saw them appear several times on the horizon, numbering some four-thousand or so. Each time they were driven to retreat when artillery fire was followed up by a fearsome Sikh cavalry charge. The conditions were hard and there is nothing like warfare for reducing a man down to his basic primal instincts. Faced with, kill or be killed, army training kicked in. When the enemy were engaged every man was expected to do his duty. It was a task that some relished as a job. I personally never wanted to kill anyone but I knew that when push came to shove, I wanted to get home, so would do whatever to survive.

Chapter Four

Death in the Orient

On the 14th August we were tasked with holding Tangkoo, a fortified place, with a ten foot high mud wall. The defensive structure proved purely ornamental to the British artillery, who battered it down to the ground. The 1st Division returned to the main base, while plans were being hatched for our advance and the taking of the Taku forts. These forts at Taku guarded the seaward approach to Tianjin, which was the route to the capital Beijing. This was to be our first major military obstacle and serious encounter with the enemy. The forts were manned by thousands of Chinese troops with at least forty-five artillery pieces at their disposal. The Chinese army knew the value of the forts strategic positions and were prepared to fight to the death to defend them. We started digging defensive trenches in preparation for an attack on the main gate. British and French guns were formed up into batteries and made ready for action at the allotted time. This was going to be the first big battle between the two forces. I thought it was going to be one hell of a fight, when it started. Now the boys of the 99th Regiment were not directly involved in the attack on the forts, but this is what happened.

At five o'clock in the morning on the 22nd August, the British and French guns opened fire upon the nearest southern fort. Those guns made a frightening noise that must have scared the life out the Chinese defenders. They pounded away relentlessly at the forts for about half an hour, then one of our shells landed in their ammunition store. There was one almighty bang, shaking the ground like an earthquake. They must have been left dazed with their ears ringing, because in the chaos their guns fell temporarily silent. It seemed like several minutes went

31

by before the Chinese gunners regained their senses, got back on their feet and remanned their guns. They took direct hits not only from the artillery but also from the gunboats out at sea. It was a brave defence but they were embarrassingly out gunned by our more modern and effective weaponry. A short time later there was a second chilling loud bang, we heard nothing. Their guns had been silenced, once and for all this time. It was a wonder anyone survived the explosion, but surprisingly they had not all been killed. It must have been a frightening thing to watch while impossible to take your eyes off at the same time.

Our commanding officer, Lieutenant-Colonel Reeves was not the kind of man to miss out on the action. His military experience secured him the job of leading the storming force of about four hundred men. This force was drawn from the Royal Marines, the 44th and the 67th regiments with our French allies. With the Chinese guns silenced the inevitable onslaught began with the British throwing scaling ladders up the walls. Brave men climbed up to the parapets meeting the Chinese in some brutal hand to hand combat. After only a relatively short time the Colours of the 67th Regiment were flying in the wind from the walls. There was no way they were coming down again. Bayonet training was put to deadly use, hundreds of Chinese soldiers were killed or wounded. Mutilated bodies were left where they fell, a trail of gore littering across the killing field. The fort was ours, the Chinese were beaten into a reluctant submission by an overwhelming battering. It was almost unbelievable that the allied forces lost just fourteen men, with fifty or so wounded, one being a young drummer boy. Lieutenant-Colonel Reeves was slightly injured with a flesh wound, but not enough to put him off carrying on.

With the Chinese artillery pieces from the first fort lost, the adrenaline filled troops now had the second fort in their sights. The second fort was about a thousand yards away across a very muddy causeway. A short time later a force from the 3rd The Buffs Regiment and the 8th Punjabi Infantry advanced towards their target. They walked into the fort without resistance, finding that about two thousand Chinese had thrown down their guns. Any military regalia identifying them as soldiers had been removed. The fate of their comrades at the first fort had obviously convinced them that resistance was futile. The captured Chinese were absolutely amazed by our mercy. We allowed them all to return to their homes and families and walk away from the conflict. Seven Victoria Crosses were awarded on that single day for feats of extreme gallantry, five to the 67th and two to the 44th Regiments.

Before the day was over, rain came down in torrents making everything through and through, soaking wet. You had to feel the pain for our battle tired and weary boys. Their road back to camp some distance away, was submerged in thick mud. The bedraggled artillery had the task of dragging the heavy guns back through it all. At times the men were knee deep, some even losing their boots. Having returned to camp, nobody had eaten anything substantial all day and they were exhausted and ravenous for food. By nightfall, their tents and belongings were drenched and they even struggled to light their fires to eat and dry out.

The initial victory was over, leaving the Chinese with a bloody nose though the end of the war was still a long way off. Our leaders were keen to enforce their advantage and demanded the Chinese Governor-General to surrender all positions up the Peiho River including the city of Tianjin, itself. The navy managed to navigate up the river with some gun boats and troops. They reached Tianjin on the 23rd August 1860 and secured the place with the minimal effort. The army then began to move up towards the city, which stood on the road giving access to the capital.

As part of the 2nd Division we commenced the march to Tianjin at the beginning of September. Taku was left under the control of the 3rd

33

The Buffs Regiment who formed a garrison. Another long march ensued from Taku to Tianjin. The road more or less followed the course of the Peiho river. Interesting houses with very well kept gardens stood on the land between road and river. The other side of the road contained endless corn fields with no trees in sight. All our senses were on stand-by and our eyes and ears, watched and listened for the slightest clue as to the enemies presence. The surface of the road was hard compacted mud not much better than a cart track. Ditches either side of the track made it impossible for the artillery guns to get off even if they wanted to. Along our journey, every now and then, we came across small villages with roof tiled houses and temples. It was an eery march with the men being on tenterhooks.

The Chinese declined to defend their fort at Beitang. We reached Tianjin unscathed in the first week of September. The navy had already secured the town prior to our arrival, so we met no resistance. This ancient place had a wall built all around it, with a gate in each side. You needed to be there to appreciate the place, it was very foreign to England but a wonder for us westerners to see.

The diplomatic mission tried to open some sort of dialogue with the Chinese, but there was no trust between the two sides and eventually it came to nothing. Consequently on the 8th September, the 1st and 67th Regiments were ordered to hold Tianjin. This was a well deserved rest for the 67th after their ordeal at Taku. The rest of us had to march on and Lieutenant-Colonel Reeves rejoined us at the head of the 99th Regiment to lead the advance. With us were two hundred marines, Barry's and Stirling's Batteries of artillery, the Kings Dragoon Guards and Fane's Sikh Horse.

The following day we marched relentlessly through the baking heat of the sun. Several of the men began flagging with sunstroke and fell to their knees. All night beer drinking had brought them down with dehydration to the point where they required being picked up for rejuvenation. It was the kind of weather where you didn't know whether to wear your sou'wester or sunhat. The road began slowly widening as we advanced along the route. This was good in one way, but corn six to ten feet tall obscured our views on either side. The curtains of vegetation had an eerie and unnerving effect, as the enemy could lie in wait and emerge without warning.

James Bruce, 8th Earl of Elgin, was the chief diplomat negotiating for the British Government. He was the High Commissioner in China and joined us at this point and met with Lieutenant General Sir James Hope Grant to discuss options.

The next day we caught sight of the elite Mongolian cavalry. There was an awkward and tense stand off, but no shots were actually fired. The Chinese commander Sengge Rinchen, was one of their top brass generals with a terrible reputation for brutality. It was an horrendous night of weather on the 10th September. The heavens opened and a violent storm erupted with torrential rain on a biblical scale. The storm must have summoned the mother of all demons up to descend on the camp. In fear, all the native Chinese attached to the column deserted and disappeared like ghosts in the night. Some of the men were freaked out by it, nobody heard any one go. There was certainly a funny atmosphere in the morning when the Chinese vanishing act was discovered. I always like to watch a good storm in progress, the power and energy is amazing. It definitely confirms that there is a greater force than mankind on earth.

Mountains near the capital came into view on the 12th September. The following day we reached Hosiwu, an old walled town on the river, where we were to wait until receiving further instructions. To be honest the regiment needed a rest and were grateful to stop for a while. Hosiwu was a virtual ghost town, almost completely deserted by the resident locals. The fact was, the Chinese were vanishing from everywhere. At some point we expected them to jump out on us, like a scene from some scary pantomime. The town did have its good points, being favourably surrounded by different types of fruit orchards. We had plenty of good food to eat anyway. The plants, trees and insects, that I observed in China were fascinating. This warring escapade was turning out to be a lesson in natural history and a botanical delight. Even in the middle of a conflict, I soaked up the scenery and absorbed the local sights, which were a wonder to see. The General decided to defend Hosiwu as a supply depot and put arrangements in place to set up a field hospital. Meanwhile the Admiral in charge of the fleet brought the artillery train up the river, escorted by detachments of troops.

After a five day rest the orders came to move on. The problem was that on the morning of the 17th September, most of the men were still heavy in drink. It was a sluggish trek at first, while the lads slowly sobered up as they marched. Make no mistake though, they were ready to fight if needed. You could have shaved with our bayonet blades, after the time we had put into sharpening them.

The main force of the attack was headed by the Cavalry Brigade, comprising of the King's Dragoon Guards with Probyn and Fane's, Sikh Horse. The combination of men and horses at the charge, instils great fear into the enemy. The artillery was made up of Stirling's half battery under Brigadier Pattle and two field batteries. The infantry was us the 99th Regiment commanded by Lieutenant-Colonel Reeves, The 2nd Regiment (Queen's) and the 15th Punjabi Infantry. Royal Marines and a detachment of Royal Engineers also came along for good measure.

So far so good as they say, but things were about to take a decisive turn for the worse. During the early hours of the 18th September 1860, a small diplomatic detachment rode out under the protection of a white flag of truce to the Chinese lines. This was in order to negotiate a safe position for our troops to camp during the talks. In the party was the diplomat, Harry Smith Parkes; Mr. Thompson, of the Commissariat

Department; Lord Elgin's private secretary, Henry Loch; Mr. De Norman, one of Lord Elgins attachés; and Mr. Thomas William Bowlby, a Times correspondent. The military escort was led by Colonel Walker, Quartermaster-General of the Cavalry Brigade. It included five men from the King's Dragoon Guards, and twenty of Fane's Horse, under the command of Lieutenant Anderson. The small diplomatic party was met by a group of high ranking Chinese officers. The discussions did not get off to a good start as there was an uneasy feeling. The diplomats sensed that the Chinese were trying to persuade us to camp in killing fields prepared for a counter attack. There was a real lack of trust between us and the Chinese. Henry Loch informed the enemy that he would have to report matters to Lieutenant General Sir James Hope Grant for his opinions. This was granted and having made his report he returned to the negotiations with Captain Brabazon, Quartermaster-General of the Royal Artillery.

The diplomats were out on a limb and the Chinese mood started to become more aggressive. Some of our men felt they were being double-crossed. Slowly the Chinese closed in surrounding them in a small place. The party became unnerved and a cloud of impending doom descended upon them. Tensions increased when a surrounded French officer was attacked by a mob. Colonel Walker, an experienced cavalry officer spotted the problem and felt compelled to ride to his aid. Walker's sword was grabbed and his hand was wounded retrieving it. Outnumbered by the crowding Chinese mob, the gravity of the situation became blatantly apparent to Walker. He realised they had been entrapped, so shouted the order to 'Charge for Your Life'. Together with all those able, he galloped at full speed for the British lines. Making their getaway, the Chinese artillery and infantry opened fire upon them. Scrambling back and reaching the lines, the furious Colonel reported the situation to Lieutenant General Sir James Hope Grant. So antagonised by the Chinese treachery, Grant ordered the immediate advance of all allied troops. It came too late to save several of the diplomat group who had been captured with a number of the military escort. Taking men under the flag of truce was seen a dastardly deed and a terrible breach of the strict codes of war.

The French advanced on the right with a squadron of the King's Dragoon Guards, supported by two of our batteries. The 99th Regiment, were quickly dispatched to support the French. The 15th Punjabi's held the centre and the 2nd Queen's Regiment and Stirling's battery held the left. The Chinese who dared to poke the beast of war had awoken it into a frenzy of rage. The Chinese mounted their attack, but each wave was ravaged by our ferocious artillery. The deadly accurate British artillery shredded their lines, time after time. The huge Chinese army had the odds stacked firmly in their favour and numbered almost thirty-thousand. Against them the British and French combined force totalled only three-thousand five-hundred.

Despite the odds, every determined Chinese cavalry charge was battered and splintered by ruthless artillery fire from our guns. As they attempted to regroup, the fierce British cavalry counter charged. The Chinese were forced to retreat and were scattered into the surrounding villages and countryside. Our lines then began to advance hunting down the stragglers and dispatching them like foxes at a hunt.

The 99th Regiment together with the 15th Punjabi Infantry advanced towards the town of Chang Chia Wan, supported by several artillery pieces. A stone bridge spanned the river leading to the gateway of this ancient walled city. We marched into the partially abandoned town with extreme caution. Our bayonets were fixed and gleaming in the sun ready for a days work. Locals who we believed posed any threat came to a swift end, tinting the shine of our weapons blood red. Some native townsfolk chose to commit suicide, anticipating that their end was nigh. Little mercy was either shown or offered during that business day of war. It was a day to be locked and shut away in that box of horrors at the back of the mind.

The Chinese had suffered a crushing blow losing almost all their artillery pieces. It sent a stark reminder of the fire power that faced them. The battle was won, but there was no time for complacency. We were still massively outnumbered by our enemy. The men of the regiment had the taste for blood and were pumped up for a killing spree.

Around the campfires that night, several of the soldiers criticised Harry Parkes foolish actions. They believed there was a time for talking and a time for fighting. With the time for talking over the fighting should be left to the army. The lads thought he had been an idiot for falling into the Chinese trap. They were agitated that valuable lives had been sacrificed by those trying to protect him.

Orders were sent to Sir Robert Napier at Hosiwu, that the 60th Regiment was to advance towards the main force. The 31st Regiment were to protect the supply route between Hosiwu and Yangtsun.

By five in the morning on the 21st September the British and French forces had reached the Eight Mile Bridge at Palikao. Our lines were formed up with the infantry on the right, artillery in the centre and cavalry on the left. The Chinese cavalry foolishly made a suicide charge on our guns. They were unmercifully cut down by an artillery barrage from a range of only two-hundred yards. Reeling from the firepower they retreated back towards their lines. The King's Dragoon Guards, supported by Fane's and Probyn's Horse chased them down and bowled into them with ruthless ferocity. Our cavalrymen were such accomplished killers, they left sabre butchered bodies littering the ground. The red earth was like the floor of an abattoir on kill day. The cavalry units skirmishes were an awesome spectacle and won the day, inflicting massive losses on the Chinese.

In comparison the infantry were using the old 'Brown Bess' muzzle loading flintlock musket. Terribly inaccurate and frustrating to use, with only an effective range of about a hundred yards. You really did have to see the 'white's of their eyes', to be in with half a chance. The only accurate part of it was the bayonet fixed to the end, so no wonder we did all that training. As the enemy retreated, Lieutenant General Sir James Hope Grant, sent the 99th Regiment with the cavalry, Marines and three Armstrong guns to follow. We were to find and neutralise any pockets of Chinese fleeing troops.

About eight miles from Beijing and close to the village of Yu-chia-wei, we unwittingly wandered into the camp of the Chinese General Paou. The mounted Dragoons were first in and came under immediate fire, taking many losses from their dug in infantry. The 99th Regiment supported by artillery were ordered in on foot. We got straight to our work of unimaginable violence, with fixed bayonets, stabbing and slicing though the Chinese at close quarters. They were dispatched like fish being gutted on a trawlers deck. Their shouts of anger, became the screams of pain and finally a silence of death. There was blood and gore everywhere to demonstrate we had earned our money for Queen and country. Nothing can prepare you for the brutality of this kind of warfare, its murderous and leaves an indelible stain on your view of humanity. I learned that day why the British chose blood red as the colour for their tunics.

In the meantime the French attacked the Palikao bridge held by the Imperial Chinese Guard. Although bravely defending the structure, they were beaten back by the French. In the action the Chinese General Paou was mortally wounded. It was supposedly during his dying breaths that he gave the orders to decapitate some of the prisoners. This cruel, selfish and needless act burned Chinese bridges for any hope of mercy from us.

Towards the end of the day as our troops prepared to encamp, the Chinese opened fire from the other side of the canal. The 15th Punjabi Infantry waded across to the other side, aggressively swarming the

Chinese like wasps. They cut their way through the Chinese, silencing their guns and slaughtering the sixty defenders. Sengge Rinchen's elite Mongolian cavalry were completely destroyed and the rest of his troops were all but defeated in the field.

After this action Lord Elgin received a message from Prince Gong the Emperor's brother, stating that he was ready to negotiate a truce. Elgin demanded the immediate release of all the prisoners and gave a three day deadline for them to respond. The following day Prince Gong sent a message stating the prisoners were all safe and well, but they would only be returned when we relinquished the Taku forts and our navy retreated back down the river. It was far too late for the Chinese to be asking for any concessions from us. None of the lads were prepared to go home until the job was properly done. Lord Elgin told them straight, they had broken all the rules of engagement by disrespecting international law and the white flag of truce. In no uncertain terms he sent a message back saying, that unless the prisoners were returned immediately, they would be subjected to the full vengeance of the British and French military. This no nonsense talk was what the lads thrived on and what they wanted to hear. Sir Robert Napier arrived on the 24th September with the reserve force comprising, the 1st Royal, the 60th Rifles and the 8th Punjabi's. All the siege guns were brought up in readiness. Needless to say, we had come to the magical point of no return.

On the 30th September the Chinese made one last ditched attempt to persuade Lord Elgin to retire his allied forces to Chang Chia Wan so a treaty could be agreed. Clown time was over with the Chinese, there was going to be no stand down of troops or any opportunity to play tricks on us. All the Chinese could do now was hope to stall us, so they could somehow regroup.

In early October, Prince Gong suggested that Harry Parkes could act as mediator in the negotiations between the two sides. Lord Elgin reiterated that no diplomatic talks could take place until all prisoners had been released unharmed. Letters arrived written in Chinese from Harry Parkes and Henry Loch. Loch cleverly made a note in Hindustani in the margin stating the letter was made under duress. This worsened any chance of diplomacy and increased the mistrust between the two sides. Two more days passed but still no prisoners had been released. Allied troops began their advance as the Chinese played their waiting game. Another letter arrived from Harry Parkes and Henry Loch giving their location as a temple by the Tey-shun gate. They were being held captive, but only three others were with them. We now had ten-thousand men camped six miles from Beijing, ready to advance on the capital on the 5th October.

The following day all troops headed for the royal Summer Palace. Somehow the British force got split from the French and while the British camped the French went on and began looting. British troops joined the French in the looting of the Summer Palace the following day. It was every man for himself, searching out and grabbing anything they thought was valuable. It was virtually a pantomime, with soldiers roaming around the rooms and corridors dressed in fine silk clothing stolen from the wardrobes of the emperor. The men became a rabble, almost out of control. Almost every inch of the palace was searched and ransacked like archaeologists looking for treasure. The Chinese must have realised any chance of compromise was now over. To placate us, Harry Parkes, Henry Loch and five French prisoners were released. Their return only served to confirm the terrible treatment and torture endured while in the custody of the Chinese. Lieutenant Anderson had become delirious and died after nine days and De Norman after two weeks. Others including Mr. Bowlby and Private Phipps from The King's Dragoon Guards were also confirmed dead.

Senior officers sought to bring the looting under control by issuing an order to the men. All prize goods taken from the Summer Palace would be collected and sold at an auction. The value raised was going to be divided equally amongst the British troops. The sale raised eight-thousand pounds and there was a further eighteen-thousand pounds from the French sale. Every British private received about four pounds in bounty. [31] The next day, Lord Elgin demanded that Prince Gong surrender the Antung Gate in the north-east of the capital. He issued an ultimatum that it would be battered down if not surrendered before twelve noon on the 13th October. Engineers using explosives were tasked to prepare to blow the gate down. The 99th Regiment and the 9th Lancers were positioned in the north-east suburbs of Beijing in readiness to storm the gate at the allotted time. On the 12th October the Chinese agreed to surrender the gate and released eight more Sikh's and one Frenchman. Again they were all terribly mistreated and in a bad condition. At noon the Chinese opened the gate allowing entry, their only option to avoid more bloodshed. Sir Robert Napier entered the city with the 67th Regiment and one-hundred men from the 8th Punjabi infantry. Two more Sikh's were released on the 14th October, one in such a poor state that he died soon after. Eight mutilated and almost unrecognisable bodies were discovered, including those of Mr. Bowdly, De Norman and Lieutenant Anderson.

With great pomp for the dead prisoners, Lord Elgin led a ceremonial funeral on the 17th October, through the city to the Russian cemetery. A spectacle of troops from all the regiments lined the streets in a show of strength, respect and outrage. There was a bad feeling about the senseless murders and tensions were high. In revenge, Lord Elgin retaliated by ordering the burning down of the Summer Palaces starting the following day. He even contemplated the total destruction of the Forbidden City in retribution for the kidnappings. Prince Gong only averted this by pleading with him and agreeing to sign a treaty.

It was a bright warm day on the 24th October as the 99th Regiment, marched into the capital Beijing as part of Lord Elgin's bodyguard. We demonstrated our military discipline parading with colours flying and drums beating. Lord Elgin's task was to complete the negotiations leading to the Treaty of Tianjin, signed between us and Prince Gong. The final treaty agreed to all our demands, including paying compensation and accepting foreign diplomats at the Imperial Qing Court in Beijing. Our regiment seized a Pekinese dog belonging to the aunt of the Chinese Emperor. We looked after the creature until we returned to England and presented it as a gift to Queen Victoria. She named it Looty, which we thought was an amusing reference to the looting. She was probably aware we nicked a fair bit from the Chinese palace. At last the war was finally over and I had managed to survive. I breathed a sigh of relief as my reward for service in China and the regiment earned the Battle honour, Pekin 1860 for its colours.

A few days later on the 9th November 1860 the 99th Regiment began the return march to Tianjin. We embarked on the HMS Bosphorus and Burlington on the 17th November 1860 destined for Canton, where we were joined by the rest of the regiment.

The regiment remained to garrison Canton for almost twelve months. It was October 1861 all companies embarked for Hong Kong and we said our final goodbyes to that distant land. China was a very foreign place in every sense of the word, completely different to the world I had known before. Many of the experiences there, I was happy to leave behind, but some especially the history and nature I banked in my memory forever and for future reference.

Chapter Five

Life in the Regiment

By the time we left Canton not much had changed at home with my family still residing in Pool Street. Benjamin Hammond was still a bricklayer and mother was earning a few quid altering and making clothes. Sarah, my sister worked as a tailoress and lived at the family home with her son William, who was being bought up by my mother. My little brother Enoch was now eleven and already working as an iron caster in a dirty foundry. I felt sorry for the lad, it was a tragedy having to work in those conditions at his age. Baby brother Abel was at school, as were my half-brothers, Benjamin and James. Thomas Bullers, Sarah's boyfriend lived with the family. He was a spur rowel maker and five years older than her. [32] Sarah married Thomas at St. Peter's and St. Paul's Church in Aston on the 16th November 1861, another family day at the church of choice. [33] I was glad they got married and everything was turning good for a change in my big sister's life. I wished I had been there to see them marry for myself.

Getting back to army life, our stay in Hong Kong was for far longer than we would have liked. The men arrived there testosterone filled from a war zone with so much pent up anger and aggression. Although in self denial they were mentally scarred by their latest experiences. They had lost the ability to relax now they were being allowed too. Some of the men were like caged animals waiting to get out. It's true what they say, the devil makes work for idle hands.

In September 1864, the lads were out as usual on the town. Most of the men were well oiled after a night of serious drinking. We bumped into another group of drunken sailors fighting with some Malays near a boarding house. There was a flashpoint, something sparked off an almighty drunken brawl, which rapidly and drastically got out of hand. Whether it was the booze or the constant humdrum, all the frustration came out resulting in four sailers being stabbed and killed. The police came out to break up the massive scrap and in panic, an Indian police officer fired from some distance away at the group. Private Lansdale from the 99th fell to the ground and died from his wounds. I managed to get the hell out of there before the police came.

The next day the crap hit the fan, but even that didn't prevent them from going out that night for second helpings. Some of the hotheads were sworn on revenge and the night ended in violence again. One police officer was killed and eleven men from the regiment were rounded up and charged with wilful murder. Senior officers came down on us like a ton of bricks, confining the regiment to barracks. Trouble rolls down hill fast, so on the 7th October the whole regiment was ordered to garrison Kowloon. This was part of the new territory conceded by the Convention of Peking, on the squalid other side of the river. We were billeted in manky huts as a punishment, well out the way of trouble in Hong Kong. The Kowloon camp was not the most sanitary place in the world, far from it. The men charged with murder were acquitted, but it didn't change anything. [34] The troops were plagued with various illnesses and nearly everyone was sick at some time. Number one company was shipped out to garrison the Taku forts, held by the British after the war, enabling trade to continue unhindered. We desperately hoped to be returning to India where most of the lads felt at home, but it was not to be. The rest of the regiment stayed at Kowloon, until the 28th February 1865. That's when HMS Tamar came to collect our beleaguered regiment together with some of the sick 67th regiment.

HMS Tamar was a brand new purpose built troop carrier, only commissioned by the navy in 1864. We were quite lucky as the well equipped ship was a lot more comfortable than the old carriers. This was the vessels first visit to the colony, but its name was to stay for years. The name Tamar was adopted for the Royal Naval base at Hong Kong, used right up until the colony was handed back to the Chinese in 1997. The ship HMS Tamar had a very good innings lasting until 1941. It was then scuttled in the Hong Kong harbour by the British to assist operations against the Japanese during World War II. The name HMS Tamar still lives on to this very day.

When we sailed destined for South Africa from Victoria Harbour at the beginning of March 1865, it was a great day. I wasn't sorry to leave the shores of these oriental lands after five long years. After the ordeal of disease and filth, we hoped to recuperate and recover. We all needed to see something fresh and different and I was looking forward to setting foot on another new continent. Army life was a free encyclopaedia of travel experiences and I was eager to add another page. [35] As the Chinese would say, 'hǎo péng you', the army had become a good friend.

Change is as good as a rest, but our passage to South Africa meant enduring the seas once again. We sailed south on the South China Sea for two thousand miles towards Jakarta on the island of East Java. This was to pick up provisions and refuel with coal to keep the engines running, for the next five thousand miles. We eventually reached Port Natal on the second week of April 1865, where we disembarked.

As soon as we got off the ship, we were back to doing what the army do best, marching! Even though, after all the time in Asia I welcomed my feet touching down for the first time in Africa. We tramped with our heavy kit all the way to Durban where we set up a camp. On the 13th April 1865 we commenced the fifty-six mile, four day trek to Fort Napier at Pietermaritzburg. South Africa was very different to China and Hong Kong both in climate and terrain, but the march was no better.

47

Natal become a British Colony in 1843 after the Boers and Zulu's were driven out of the area. The British introduced plantations of sugar and cotton with workers brought in from India. This wasn't exactly to the native Africans liking, so we were there protecting British interests in the newly procured lands. The Cape was hot and sweaty, but far better than China and definitely more healthy. Over the next few years we saw a fair bit of movement around the Cape Town province. This was mainly to demonstrate our ability to be everywhere at the same time. It was the art of eluding the natives into believing the British presence was bigger than it actually was.

The highlight of this tour came on the 31st December 1868, when the colony received a visit from a very important guest, HRH Prince Alfred, Duke of Edinburgh, the queen's second son. Due to his surprise arrival to inspect the regiment we were put through our paces. The corporals almost lost their voices with all the shouting they did in preparation. You have heard the phrase spit and polish, the whole place stunk of it. We had everything gleaming almost to perfection ready for the prince's perusal. The Prince had arrived from England as commander of HMS Galatea for New Year. He came to the camp and played and lost a game of cricket with our officers. Then came the parade, where he moved slowly along the ranks, trying to find something wrong. He could not help but be impressed by out turnout and said that he would never forget that day and hoped to see us all again sometime soon. It was an honour and privilege to be there and we all thought that he would be good to his word. From that day forward, Prince Alfred certainly took a great personal interest in the 99th Regiment. 36 37

In early summer 1869, we received our orders about returning to England. I suppose we had done our bit and it was somebody else's turn in Africa. On the 26th July, over five hundred of us, including some officers wives and kids boarded HMS Orontes to begin the nine thousand mile journey home. As we sailed away I realised another four years had passed and another continent was disappearing from my view maybe forever. At least I was returning to good old England, to some sort of normality! To be honest I was looking forward to making it back to home soil. Mother would be glad to hear of my return at any rate.

Making a short stop at St. Helena on the 4th August we sailed on. Not too far distant afterwards the ship developed a serious problem when the engine stopped working properly. We managed to limp the vessel to the Ascension Island using the rigging and sails for an emergency stop. We arrived at the island port on the 12th August 1869. A navy diver went down and found the screw was damaged and could not be repaired in situ. While decisions were being made all the wives and children went ashore. On the island the children became unwell with raging temperatures, sore throats and rashes all over their skin. The ships surgeon diagnosed scarletina, a major killer of children. One hundred and eighty-two, men, women and children stayed behind when we set off again on 17th August. I don't think it would have been fair to drag the kids back with us as they would not have made it. I hoped and prayed the poor souls did get home.

The navy had sent out HMS Perseus a sloop ship that had been tasked with shadowing our broken ship to Plymouth. It turned out to be a terrible voyage where we encountered a two day storm of gale force proportions. The tempest made even the men with cast iron stomachs feel sick and fear for their lives. In calmer periods of the voyage HMS Perseus towed us towards home, to speed things up. From Plymouth we were towed to Portsmouth, arriving the last week in September. The homecoming journey was a bit of an anti climax as we limped in. However, general excitement erupted when the lads spotted Portsmouth harbour approaching. Cheers rang out, such was the desperation to get back on home ground. [38]

I had been away for ten long years, I left a naive sixteen year old lad who thought he knew everything. I returned a twenty-six year old man, who realised there was still an awful lot to learn. I certainly wasn't the same person, you can't un-see or undo what has happened. I was now a man of the world, a senior private in the ranks and that brought status and respect. I was no longer at the bottom and people looked up to me.

After disembarking our beleaguered vessel we were marched to the beat of the drums, through the town towards the Grange and Gomer forts at Gosport. These moments are always a proud time and there is nothing like a bit of pageant to brighten up the day. On the march one of the lads, Private Murphy collapsed. We all thought he had fainted from the ordeal on the boat, but later found out the twenty-eight year old single man, had died. The doctor said it was apoplexy that killed him, guess his time had come! Sometimes there is no rhyme or reason to life, he was stuck down in his prime, such a waste. [39]

At the end of March 1870 we were transferred over to the Isle of Wight. Queen Victoria had been a widow and virtual recluse since Prince Albert's death in 1861. The prince had built Osborne House for her and the family and I suppose she found it sentimental and comforting. She spent most of her time at the property and as a result the military presence was maintained for Her Majesty's protection.

As the 61st Regiment left for their new quarters at Dublin we moved into Albany Barracks on the island. In April 1870, I was one of the soldiers selected to be sent to East Cowes as a Guard of Honour for the Queen. We were there for the duration of time the Queen was in residence at Osborne House. It was a rare honour to directly serve your queen, even though I had worn her uniform for over ten years. Queen Victoria stayed on the island until her court moved to Windsor Castle in August. Several important people visited the queen on a regular basis, so we had to be on guard all of the time. Lieutenant-General, George Upton, 3rd Viscount Templeton, commanding army officer for the Portsmouth district came to inspect us in October. The top brass needed to feel important by keeping us on our toes, they also liked to impress the Queen. In February 1871 the regiment had its numbers fixed at six-hundred rank and file and as a result some of the men took the opportunity to leave the regiment. Our tour of duty on the island was coming to a conclusion and we were returning to Aldershot. We arrived back at Aldershot on the 2nd June 1871. My military career had turned one full circle, I was back where I started, this time camping in the Guards enclosure at the base. I started to think the curtains were slowly closing on my military career, but there were still a few highlights to come, just before I went.

Excitement sky rocketed on Monday the 7th August 1871, when Prince Albert, Duke of Edinburgh visited the regiment at Aldershot. The more senior men had not forgotten the time he inspected the regiment in Africa. He promised to see us again on that occasion and he had not failed to keep the pledge he made. He came this time to present our new regimental colours. As the band played, we all marched while our old colours were trooped for the final time. The Prince rode on to the parade ground with a detachment of the 12th Lancers. I savoured that moment in time with great pride. I watched as the new colours were ceremonially draped over the drums and consecrated by the regimental chaplain. His Royal Highness received the new colours and formally handed them over to our ensigns.

He spoke to the men, confirming his visit was to fulfil his promise made at the Cape of Good Hope to see us again. He said the 99th Regiment held his highest regard and respect in all the British army. He made a joke about him being a naval officer and hoped we didn't think less of him for it. The whole regiment applauded him for his kind words. He was sure the regiment would guard the new colours as bravely as they did the old ones, where ever they travelled in the world. The Prince concluded by saying, 'May glory and honour ever attend you and your colours'. Our commanding officer, Colonel John Hart Dunne then said a few words. He said, the old colours were presented to the regiment thirty years ago and had since visited many distant colonies, known to the prince. With the officers and new colours at the front, we marched past the prince giving the Royal Salute in columns. This concluded the days ceremony in a very satisfying way to everyone who attended. The prince continued to support the regiment culminating in 1874, when it was renamed as the 99th Duke of Edinburgh's Regiment.[40]

I had begun to think it would be nice to get home and start a new life with a wife and family. Some of the lads did have wives in tow, but I never thought it was right to drag them around whenever the army called. I had one more spectacle to see before I hung up the musket and boots.

More or less the whole Royal Family visited Aldershot on the 5th July 1872, when we were greatly honoured by the Queen coming to inspect the division. The royal party included, the Prince and Princess of Wales, the Duke of Cambridge, the Duke of Edinburgh, Prince Arthur, Prince Leopold and Princess Beatrice. They all arrived by train just before two o'clock in the afternoon, to a greeting of rapturous applause and flag waving. The whole town was out for the spectacle and all the shops had been closed for the day. No one wanted to miss out on a chance of seeing the queen up close. The 7th Hussars provided the royal escort and General Sir Hope Grant, our commander-in-chief in China, greeted the royals on arrival. There was a great atmosphere about the place with a sense of real excitement. To top it, the royals came on a slightly breezy, bright sunny day.

In the afternoon the Queen and her party arrived at Long Valley. Whilst the band played the National Anthem, we marched past the saluting base on the steeple chase course whilst giving the Royal Salute. The infantry were the last in the line of troops stretching about a mile long. Following the 82nd Regiment, we marched in accordance with our reputation, steady and precise at quick time, in double companies. I have to say, we pulled it off yet again as expected. The Long Valley grass was in our favour, firm from the previous week of sunshine. A simulated attack from the north was the finale for the day. This was to be a demonstration of epic magnitude designed to impress our distinguished guests. At about seven o'clock in the evening, her majesty decided to leave the field. The day appeared to have tired the queen and she headed home just before eight o'clock with Princess Beatrice and Prince Leopold in tow. The rest of the royals remained until events concluded and afterwards were entertained by the guards. The last royals left Aldershot from the South Western Railway station shortly before nine o'clock destined for London. It was a proper royal occasion, all in all, with seventeen thousand troops, two thousand horses and fifty-two guns taking part. Not a bad turnout to show off to the Queen! [41]

The autumn manoeuvres started on Tuesday the 10th September, with all regiments attending. On Thursday at Beacon Hill, there was a royal march past overseen by the Prince of Wales. The total number of men involved was just short of thirty-thousand, including the militia regiments. Several foreign military officers and Japanese ambassadors spectated the whole days event. The 99th Regiment once again out matched the best of regiments with their turnout and marching prowess. [42]

On the 16th September me and the regiment rolled out of Aldershot on the train to Shorncliffe Barracks in Kent. This was to be my last posting with the British Army. I applied to leave the army on the 5th November 1872 and this was granted three days later. I was officially discharged on the 18th November 1872. It was an emotional day saying my final goodbyes to the men I had served with and who had become my family. I served for thirteen years, one hundred and seventeen days with the colours. I finally headed home, what ever that meant, to start the next chapter in my life. [43]

Chapter Six

The Homecoming!

S ince I left Walsall in 1859, things had moved on. My mother was now fifty-one years of age and lived with her husband Benjamin Hammond, in a small courtyard house off Ablewell Street. My youngest brother Abel, was nineteen and worked as a plater, while half-brothers, Benjamin and James were both casters in a foundry. Edward, my youngest half-brother was at school. [44] My sister Sarah, lived with her husband Thomas Bullers in Cemetery Walk, with her fourteen year old son William. [45] Living with her was my twenty-two year old brother Enoch. He was employed as a brass and German silver plater. I left Walsall to avoid the factories, but returned to find that all of my family had resigned themselves to the filth just to earn a living. They had been entrapped by their surroundings but were still a very close knit family who looked out for each other.

I handed my kit bag to the quarter master at Shorncliffe with a hint of sadness. This was the last formality before being discharged from Her Majesty's Service. I made the journey back to Walsall alone, which gave me plenty of time to reflect on what I would find when I returned. I thought a lot about the people I left behind in the old streets and the poverty they suffered. It took several hours and trains before I heard the guard shouting Walsall! I looked out to see a strangely familiar platform emerge from the steam and smoke, I had landed back in my home town. I reminisced about how my dad helped build this station back in his day. I walked down the platform and out into a dark Station Street, there was no one about to greet me. To be fair, nobody actually knew what time I was coming anyway, so I could not expect the flags to be out. It occurred to me that I had probably changed so much physically, people would not have known me anyway. After all I was sixteen when I left, just a boy, yet here I was at twenty-nine a battle hardened veteran from the army. I was at the peak of my physical fitness and had a well developed no nonsense character forged by army life. The Walsall local twang I left with, had mellowed living with people from all over. I probably looked and sounded like a bit of an outsider with my clean and tanned complexion. I felt so different as well, I had been somewhere and done something. I had served and seen the Queen up close, not just on a coin or stamp. The lights were on in the alehouses as I walked down Park Street towards the bridge and noise spilt out from them onto the footpath. Casting a passing glimpse towards the voices, I carried on walking up the High Street towards St. Matthew's church at the top of the hill. It was quite an eerie feeling, like seeing the ghost of an old friend appear before you. I was really looking forward to seeing my mother again after all this time. I wanted to tell her a little bit about my time away, although I knew it was too late. I did at least have money in my pocket thanks to the army, which is more than I had when I left. When the steps of Church Hill came in sight, I realised how little the place had changed during my absence, which was strangely comforting. I reached mothers house, but decided to let them be for the night. I popped into the Barley Mow for a quick pint of local ale. I walked in followed by the sound of silence, like a foreigner had been detected amongst their midst. My voice added suspicion as I spoke to order my drink at the bar. The landlord asked me if I was new in town, so I told him I was returning from my time in the army. He relaxed when I said I was born in Walsall and my mother lived around the corner. I decided to treat myself to some lodgings for a night of rest.

The next day, I went to see mother with mixed but joyous feelings. It was a great feeling seeing her after so long, although time had not been kind to her. The face I remembered was the same, except for the lines drawn by the passing of time. She was, as always still a delight to see and I hugged and kissed her brow. She was on her own and embraced me as only a mother could. She looked at me to take in how much I had changed, but I think she saw the ghost of my father in my image. She transfixed on my face and was almost hypnotised by my presence until I broke the silence. I was quite tall, strong with broad shoulders and quite different to the rest of my siblings. I was confident and possessed bearing, I could see she was proud of me and in return I was thankful of the sacrifices she had made to get the family through. We sat for about an hour and talked about the family. She told me that Abel was getting married next month, I felt I was being welcomed home, there was a sense of family belonging which had been missing for some time. Mum was the power that held everyone together, the one people turned to for advice and guidance.

I soon got some casual labouring work outdoors in the building industry and was relatively well off. I was determined never to work in the factories, that was a line I was not going to cross.

The whole family turned out at St. Matthew's church on Sunday the 8th December 1872, for the wedding of Abel my youngest brother. [46] Abel was twenty-one and his new wife Emma Bird was twenty-nine. It was good to see them all, although I did get the sense that I was being treated with a bit of suspicion by some members of the family. I suppose I had changed quite a bit, I was different, even a little menacing as they had heard about some of my military exploits. Perhaps I was reading too much into things, maybe I was experiencing a little bit of aspergers. I had after all been away for a long time.

At Abel's wedding, I caught sight of a young lady called Elizabeth Sharratt. She was a local girl who was lodging at the Paddock and working as a press operator. She was younger than me, very mature and beautiful and we struck up a conversation. I saw people looking at me, probably thinking, he's only been back two minutes and already after the girls. We agreed to meet each other to walk out, it was the start of a fine romance. After all that time away, I was ready to meet someone special. I couldn't see the point in beating around the bush, so after a short time I asked Elizabeth for her hand. To my delight she instantly said yes, bagging one of the most eligible bachelors in working class circles. After a whirlwind romance, three months later on the 17th February 1873 we married at St. Peter's and St. Paul's Church, Aston. [47] [48] It was my mothers idea to marry at Aston so we told the vicar we lived there to make her happy. We made it a bit of a family outing, nothing special or flashy but a great day nonetheless. My sister Sarah and her husband Thomas were our witnesses. The family always liked a day out in Aston and a ride on the train down the old Grand Junction line!

It was sometime in June 1873 that I bumped into the old copper, Police Constable Childs. He was the man who had advised me to join the army all those years ago. He was now a sergeant and had been in the police since 1854. He seemed to be genuinely pleased that I had seen the world and delighted in my story about what I had seen and done. He said he was glad I took his advice and was happy he was able to help. He recommended Walsall Borough Police as a career for me, saying they were looking for good men. The work was steady with good benefits and beat working in the factories. He said it was ideal for ex-military men who knew how to handle difficult situations. I told him that I would have a think about it, but it did seem to tick a few boxes. He said if I was interested, he would put a good word in with the superintendent. It was a nice invitation and I knew he would help me get the job if I wanted it. I discussed the prospect with Elizabeth and decided I was up for it. I went for an interview with superintendent, John Wyatt Cater. He was a man who had risen through the police ranks, a no nonsense kind of bloke, firm but fair. He asked about my time in the army and seemed to warm to me. He offered me the job that day saying that he wanted me to start straight away. One of the more experienced lads was going to be showing me the ropes. I guess the interview went well. So here I was, back in uniform once again, this time black instead of the bright red but just as uncomfortable and stiff.

On the 7th July 1873 another family knot was tied when my brother Enoch got married to Mary Jane Carpenter at St. John's church, Pleck. [49] I was very close to Enoch and my wife Elizabeth and me were the witnesses at his wedding. Everything went well but I had a strange feeling about half-brothers Ben and Jim. They knew I had joined the police and viewed me with even more suspicion than usual. Jim was the one with all the attitude and presence about him, he was polite enough in a cheeky kind of way, but I had a funny feeling about him. I asked mother if everything was all right, she told me it was just his way. She was always the peace maker, I knew they were not keen on me being a constable, but didn't realise at that time how much of a problem it was. I had been away for a long time and did not really know my half-brothers very well at all.

I soon settled into policing, they were a good bunch, some of the men from the army like me. I suppose soldiers knew how to take orders and do things in a certain way, which suited the police. Walsall was the same as any town in England, it had its fair share of trouble and strife. Variety is the spice of life and trouble was no stranger to me. The heavy industries had attracted a rough type of people to the area. Drinking had increased and general moral standards had gone down. After dark, the town was a very different place, it was the time the ne'er do wells roamed the streets looking for mischief. I worked day and night shifts, the work was never the same two days on the trot. You never knew who or what to expect around every corner. It was a real eye opener as to how the old place was changing.

One of my jobs was taking the people I had arrested to court and prosecuting the cases before the magistrates. In those days the court was often attended by the superintendent who watched us giving evidence. One of my first cases was a fight between two women, Bridget Kelly and Mary O'Brien in Wolverhampton Lane. The one woman had battered the other one resulting in her arrest for the assault. She went before the court the next day and I attended to give evidence. The magistrates seemed to take my every word as gospel and needed no further evidence to prove her guilty. She was fined ten shillings plus costs, a small fortune or in default fourteen days in prison. Justice was certainly severe and costly! [50]

On the 29th March 1875, I was in the parade room at Walsall police station when the sergeant came over to speak with me. He told me there was a very important job he required to be carried out to the letter. A man who had been found guilty of murder at Stafford was due for hanging in the morning. At first I thought he was blagging, but the serious look on his face told me he was either a good liar or he was being deadly serious. Apparently the regular hangman, William Marwood was unavailable due to a neck stretching double-booking. I thought for a split second, he was going to ask me how I was fixed to jump into the role. He then told me the county had recently appointed a new hangman, named George Incher from Dudley. Incher had a bit of form in policing terms and he also liked a drink or two. It's fair to say that his reliability was in question and my job was to meet him at Walsall railway station and take him directly to Stafford gaol to complete his task. The sergeant said, if I messed it up, not to bother coming back, so no pressure!

When George Incher stepped down from the Dudley train on the Walsall platform, I was waiting for our meeting. His dusky figure wearing a tatty dark hat and carrying a small leather bag shuffled towards me. As he got closer, I saw the whites of his eyes and the aged contours of his face and general unkempt appearance. In fact he looked worse than a tramp and smelt like one as well. My time with the 99th

Regiment, the elite, meant I knew a shower of shit when I saw one and he was definitely one. His gruff voice asked if I was there for him and I confirmed I had orders to escort him to Stafford. We boarded the Stafford train and waited for the whistle to blow. The sudden shunt of the engine and the tug of the carriage signalled the start of our journey. This was a real life ghost train into the ghoulish unknown. Incher had the smell of booze on his breath, you could tell he had been drinking and he said he couldn't wait to get it over with. I don't think he was worried about his grim task, he didn't strike me as a man with a conscience. It was more likely he anticipated his payout to further his alcoholic experience. He was an almost sad character, straight off the pages of a Dickens novel. He had a vacant stare, an expressionless face and a deep but quiet monotone voice. Although he appeared to be slow and almost inactive, he had the awkward air of unpredictability. I watched his every move for signs of a sudden and unexpected movement, but none came. To be honest he was probably more drunk than I thought. I came to the conclusion that his demeanour was worn as a cloak to hide his lack of sobriety.

We made the short slow walk from the railway station to Stafford gaol at the top of the town. The place loomed more like a castle than a prison with its arched gatehouse and towers. On arrival, the warders were expecting us, they always expected the hangman to turn up the day before an execution. Catching sight of Incher they were equally as unimpressed by his turn out as me. Word was sent to the governor, who was horrified, if not surprised by the report. He immediately sent urgent orders instructing his men to fetch a new set of clothes.

Some dignitaries were invited to witness the execution and Incher was expected to look the part when officiating the next day. I stayed at Stafford gaol that night a place you would not frequent by choice. That evening I had conversations with the prison guards about the murder case and the story of the man being executed in the morning. The events had been published in all the local papers and were about a twenty-two year old named John Stanton. Oddly the convicted mans cousin, also John Stanton, was one of the senior warders at the gaol. Sadly, Stanton's pregnant wife Sarah had visited him earlier in the day. She would never see him alive again and the unborn child would never see his father. She married Stanton when she was just seventeen in the August of 1874. The marriage was a disaster waiting to happen, Stanton was already a convicted thief and by all accounts a violent man and a heavy drinker. [51]

This grizzly saga took place at the Dog and Partridge public house in the Backwalls of Stafford on the 17th January 1875. [52] On that fateful night Stanton and his uncle Thomas Nield were drinking together at the pub. The mood changed when Nield mocked his young nephew, whose mind was distorted with drink, clouding his judgement. The argument was nothing more than a squabble about some washing, but Stanton was unhinged. He stormed out of the pub in a rage of madness, stumbling along to the door of his workshop just down the road. Reaching a razor sharp blade from the top of his workbench, he muttered words of revenge under his breath. Making the short return distance back to the Dog and Partridge, he concealed the weapon within his coat. Stanton's small figure entered the doorway of the pub from the cold street, hiding his true thoughts from the others. With a cool look on his face he sat down, fooling his uncle Thomas into thinking he was making things good between them. As Thomas raised his glass in conciliation to Stanton, he pulled the knife from his pocket and plunged it deep into his uncle's chest piercing his heart. The people around him gasped in disbelief and the landlady screamed at him, "What you done John?". He immediately got up and left, throwing the blood stained knife into the yard of a nearby property. Nield was to die from the stab wound before the night was over. This was the mad and senseless killing of a defenceless relative in cold blood for nothing more than a few badly

61

chosen words of mockery. Stanton was arrested the following day and tried for wilful murder. At the Staffordshire Lent Assizes on the 10th March 1875 after hearing all the evidence, the Judge only needed four minutes to consider the case and find him guilty. Then donned in his black cap, the Judge delivered the only sentence available to him. The death sentence of hanging by the neck until he was dead.

Early on the morning of the execution, Incher got up and got dressed in his new clothes, almost looking the part. Stanton was visited by the chaplain who gave him the sacraments of holy communion. Incher pinioned Stanton's arms, before leading him out of the condemned cell. The procession then commenced, led by the under-sheriff, surgeon, deputy-governor and chaplain. Stanton was closely followed by the shadowy figure of Incher and an escort of prison officers. I had seen bodies hanging before but never attended an execution. I remember thinking it was a very formal occasion, almost ceremonial. Stanton looked pale as he was walked along the crunching gravel path to the prison square. It was here they had erected the gallows to stage the event. A short religious service took place and then the lame Stanton, clumsily climbed the scaffold steps. The last words I heard him say were, "Lord have mercy upon me be merciful to me sinner". Incher placed the rope around Stanton's neck tied with a distinctive hangman's noose. He then placed a white canvas bag over his head to hide his feeble face from view. He shuffled the few steps back to the lever mechanism designed to open the trap door. There he paused in a frozen stillness and gripped the bolt of the drop in readiness with white knuckles. Almost mechanically when the prison timepiece struck eight o'clock, Incher yanked the bolt sending Stanton into free fall, ending with a dull thud. His body continued to twitch and jerk for what seemed like an eternity to some morbid silent rhythm only heard by him. His death came slowly as the rope gradually squoze tight, choking and throttling him by cutting off his last gasps for air. The audience watched for his much anticipated last movement. Then a chilling silence descended like a mark of final respect. Justice had been done in a very brutal, decisive and terminal way. I suppose in life we all want justice and the authorities there to protect us, to carry it out. It was still a ruthless spectacle to watch. The last public hanging was only seven years before, when great crowds would gather to get ring side seats. It's not the most attractive part of human nature to want to participate in brutal acts of violence even as a spectator. The funny thing was both Incher and Stanton were cordwainers, that's the old term for shoe makers. Standing side by side, not many would pick Stanton as the murderer out of the two men. That just goes to show you can't judge a book by its cover. [53]

My sergeant only told me to get Incher to Stafford, there was no mention of getting him back. He had after all been paid and didn't seem keen to come back to Walsall with me. His sombre work was done and he didn't feel the need to be sober as well. He vanished into the town for some alcoholic sustenance, to erase his memory and to disinfect his conscience of the days events. When the gate of the prison opened to let me out, I bid farewell to the guards. There was a great sense of relief as the whole experience had been very claustrophobic. I saw no time had been wasted in pinning the public notice to the outside of the prison gate, confirming that the hanging had taken place.

Looking to the freedom outside, my attention was drawn to a slim young woman standing in the street. Our eyes met as the guard told me it was Stanton's widow, Sarah. She was a good looking girl with kind eyes, but you could tell she had suffered from the whole saga. As I walked away in my authoritative policeman's way, I could not help but feel her pain. After all she had no part in the crime, she was a victim and was now alone with a child on the way. The thought crossed my mind, maybe she went there that morning to see the official confirmation of her freedom from a cruel husband.

The fragility of life was an essence that frequently floated in the air of human existence. The fragrance of death visited my nostrils only a short time after witnessing Stanton's execution. It was almost like God was punishing me for being in someway involved. Illness struck my young and beautiful wife Elizabeth and she began failing fast. The doctor was powerless to prevent the uterine disease, a cancer, draining her of all strength in an intolerable and painful way. I held her in my arms as her last spark of life was wrenched away from her on the 7th June 1875. [54] She was just twenty-four years old, far too young to have left this world. Her passing plunged me into a world of unbelievable painful grief. While desperately trying to hide the torment, I knew I was papering over a deep crack. I had to lock it away to prevent the whole thing consuming me with grief. Emotional pain is so personal, no one can feel it for you. There are no outside clues to show how bad it really is, other than unexplained odd behaviour. Time heals all ills they say, so if you stay alive it should get better! The whole thing tested my very faith, mum told me that when the Lord can't come himself he will always send to those who wait.

At Elizabeth's funeral, mother and Enoch stayed by my side and walked with me as we left the churchyard. Neither Jim or Ben gave me any problems, mother had given her instructions, she had to be obeyed and asserted her demands by just giving them a motherly look. I reckon they had all received a look that day, or maybe they really did feel my pain. I wondered what the hell I had done to deserve it, but life continued and I threw myself at my work in an attempt to make it go away. I had been robbed in the cruelest of ways. I realised how mum must have felt when she found out dad was gone.

Over the next few weeks or so, I walked and functioned on pure inherent fibre running through my very core. I almost robotically continued until the light of day once again emerged as my saviour. The Lord really does act in mysterious ways, mother was right, yet again.

Whilst out on foot patrol around the town, I saw who I thought was Sarah Stanton on a number of occasions. I thought I was going insane seeing her eyes glancing at me, just the same as they did outside Stafford gaol on that fateful day. It was like a haunting dream, we never spoke and she just vanished into the crowd and away from my view. Why would a girl from Stafford be in Walsall anyway? As time went on I could see the girl was pregnant and I knew it was Sarah. I decided to make it my job to stop and ask when I saw her next. I did not have long to wait, soon after I saw her again in Digbeth at the bottom of the market. She froze like a statue when she saw me purposely walking over towards her. I stopped in front of her and asked if she was Sarah Stanton. She looked apprehensive but instantly remembered that I was the policeman from Stafford. It turned out she was a Walsall girl who had met Stanton when he came the town picking up leather supplies for his shoemaking. After the execution, she returned to be near her family. She also wanted to escape the hassle and aftermath of her husbands dreadful reputation. He left her a vulnerable pregnant widow, alone to fend for herself. She had no family or friends in Stafford and she did not want to be constantly reminded that she was a murderers wife. Her mother had died a few years earlier but her father still lived in Church Street. She also had seven sisters living around the area. Her son, who she named Robert after her father, was born in late summer 1875. Sadly for her, a short time later her father died. [55] [56]

We met and spoke a few times while she was doing her shopping and I was patrolling the marketplace. It was more a case that we were actually seeking each other out. I could feel an unexplainable bond had been made between us, drawing us slowly together like the poles of a magnet. I couldn't help but wonder, why and how our lives had crossed in this way. Maybe it was because we both suffered emotional trauma in our lives or was it written in the stars. Who knows but Kismet, determined we were destined to be together after hitting it off straight away. I was thirty-two and she was just eighteen, though it didn't seem to matter. I think we were both searching for something in our lives, she wanted someone to feel safe with and I just wanted her. She was beautiful and had ridden out life's cruel storm and emerged surprisingly and wonderfully unbroken from it. She was searching for a knight in armour and I for a nurse for my troubled mind. She never mentioned her dead husband, it was as if she had wiped his memory from her mind. I suppose it was part of her survival mechanism. I always wondered if he ever beat her, but she was too proud to talk about it, even if he did. The monstrous man's memory had been put into a drawer in her mind, which she firmly closed and locked. I respected her wish, I certainly didn't want to release the devil she had locked away forever. I did fear that young Robert would one day ask for the truth about his father, but knew that would be a long way off.

I told my mother that I was going to marry Sarah and she asked about the child, Robert. I assured her that Robert would be bought up as my son and she gave her approval. I obviously didn't need her say so, but it was a good feeling having her on my side. She was never really bothered about protocols or beliefs, just the happiness of her family. If Sarah made me happy, then that was all she was bothered about.

On a Sunday night in the middle of October, I was on duty with Police Constable Barber in Lower Rushall Street. We heard some strange noises coming from nearby shops. As we turned the corner we saw two drunks, Joseph Richardson and John Gilligan ripping the shutters off some of the shops fronts. We grabbed hold of them and took the details of the unruly duo. At court they found a witness to say they were both sober and completely denied being responsible. The bench were not fooled and both were fined twenty shillings and costs or in default fourteen days imprisonment. [57]

Our wedding day was set for the 22nd November 1876 at St. Michael's church, Rushall. [58] Mother asked if I would consider getting married at Aston, but I told her it would be too painful and she understood my reason. I was living in James Street at the time, now called Leckie Road. I decided to ask my eldest half-brother, Ben Hammond to be one of our witnesses. Mother persuaded me, because she wanted the two sides of the family to come closer together. I couldn't blame her for wanting that, she sensed there was a little tension between me and my half-brothers, especially Jim. In those days weddings were fairly informal affairs, nobody had money to throw around. The wedding was a great success with everybody behaving, which was unusual for the Hammond's.

Policing business certainly showed me the good and bad sides of life. In May 1877, I went to a woman being beaten by a drunken man called Mark Moffatt at the top end of Park Street, the rough end of town. As I got there he was ripping the hair out of her head by the roots and giving her a proper nasty kicking. On seeing me he decided to run to the house, but I was already after him. He grabbed a claw hammer and threateningly shouted he was going to cave my head in. His eyes were fully glazed over when I ordered him to put his weapon down. He was so crazed, he wasn't interested in any easy resolution. He wanted things to be the hard way and swung the weapon from side to side as I approached. It wasn't the bayonet training I was used to, but I screamed the war cry at him as I'd been taught and the shock made him stop for a split second. As he hesitated, I gave him a sharp blow to the ribs and one to the head. His miserable fight was over and the handcuffs were secured. The poor woman had taken a horrible beating, which by all accounts was completely unprovoked. Whatever she might have done, did not deserve that terrible treatment, it was undefendable behaviour. He went up before the Magistrates on Monday morning, still sporting the bruises he got for resisting arrest on the way to the cells. The chairman called him inhuman and instantly gave him two months with hard labour. Prison was not easy, but for what he did to her, he should have got six months. The magistrates did not like men beating women, this was Victorian values and females were ladies of the fairer sex. [59]

I was determined to bring up Sarah's boy Robert as my own son, he was a great kid and caused me very little trouble. He reminded me so much of her that I'm sure he inherited all her good qualities and none of his fathers. Our first child together, William Henry was born on the 30th November 1877. [60] He was a fine lad who looked a lot like me and his coming made me understand what family life was all about. He was the first of twelve children we were going to have over the next twenty years, seven girls and five boys, with two of the girls twins.

I gained a lot of respect around the town for being fair with the local people I dealt with. At the end of the day, I lived amongst these people, there were some bad ones, but they were mostly good. Policing was all about understanding and having the discretion to deal with things in a fair way. The theory of policing by consent had been born and it was the bedrock of the profession for years to come. The only time that anyone had a beating from me was if they insisted on it, that is, they threatened violence or struck out first. After all I was wearing the uniform and that commanded respect. To be fair, most people accepted a beating if they knew they deserved one, that was just the way it was. The law was the law and it had to be obeyed or you were punished for it, that was my job. Firm, fair, friendly and just, that was my motto and it seemed to work!

Embarrassingly but not surprisingly for me, a few people started to give me the word that Jim Hammond, my half-brother was up to all sorts and thought I should know about it. The fact was, I did know he was building up a reputation for being a wide boy in the back alleys of the town. The problem was he was a clever and cunning kid, who had a way of getting the ear of people and persuading them to do things he wanted. Unfortunately, he was hell bent on breaking as many laws as he could along the way. He got away with most things, much to the delight of the people who took a share of his ill gotten gains. Jim was a villain, a rogue who enticed people along, they looked up to him as if he was a local hero, perhaps he was in their eyes. He had a very convincing character and talked the talk. He could also look after himself and never shied away from a fight to prove a point. Jim wasn't exactly a hard man, but had a reputation to keep up amongst his peers and entourage. Ben was always at his side to add extra muscle when needed, but always seemed to follow Jim's lead.

After getting away with things for some time, Jim was caught poaching early April 1878. He was seen by a young lad named Alfred Allen, running a hare with two dogs on land belonging to Mr. Moore. He appeared at Rushall Police Court on the 22nd April 1878 charged with game trespass. He denied the offence claiming that he was in Lichfield that morning. He brought a witness, Frederick Riley from Stafford Street, who said he had been with him in Lichfield. The magistrates dismissed Riley's evidence and considered the case proved. Jim was fined ten shillings and costs or fourteen days imprisonment. He was furious about getting a ten bob fine, but accepted the risks he was taking. It was a bit awkward having your brother before the magistrates, but nobody said much at the police station. There was a saying, you can choose your friends, but not your family and that summed it up. They all knew, me and Jim didn't get on that well and he was heading off the rails. It was almost like he had a rebellious point to prove with me and rules in general. He had no regard for authority and was beyond being changed by reason. [61] [62] [63] [64]

Policing at the time was a dangerous game. Some of the parishioners relished on a good argument or fight to sort disputes out between themselves. I'm not just talking about the men, the women were just as bad, in fact there was no stopping them once they started. In the summer of 1878, I was heading back to the police station when I heard a woman screaming at the top of her voice. I found that the screeching was coming from Freer's Yard, a courtyard of small houses running off from an alleyway on High Street. These places were like rat traps, once you were in these courts you were in. The wailing woman, Mary Doyle was rat faced drunk almost hysterical, I tried everything to calm her down but got nowhere. My words were like pouring fuel on the fire of her frustration with the world. Exhausting all other options, in the end I had to arrest her. As soon as I took hold of her, another drunken woman Mary Silk ran over like a banshee, beckoning for others to help them. Within seconds there was an uncontrollable mob around me, grabbing and pushing and my hat was knocked off with a brick. I grabbed hold of my whistle and blew it with all my might, summoning help from the police station, which was luckily just around the corner. The boys arrived like the Sikh cavalry, dispersing the rowdy bunch back into their hovels, with the exception of the two women involved. Kicking and screaming obscenities they were dragged to the office and given accommodation at Her Majesty's hotel. After a night in the cool cells they awoke to a sober reality of what happened the night before. Both were totally apologetic for their behaviour, which was a normal reaction after the event. The magistrates had no sympathy and ignored their expressions of sorrow. Silk was fined five shilling for obstructing a constable and Doyle two and a half shillings for being drunk and disorderly. The message soon got around the streets of Walsall warning others not to obstruct the police. [65]

A sad dark cloud drifted over the inhabitants of Walsall during the Christmas of 1878. It was Christmas Eve when awful news spread that the towns nursing hero Sister Dora, had died. She was just forty-six years old when her own personal battle with breast cancer was lost. Dorothy Pattison was not a local girl, but she had been wholeheartedly adopted by the townspeople as one of their own. Her much appreciated deeds of kindness and care had made such a difference to alleviate some of the suffering of the working classes.

Her funeral procession began at two o'clock on Saturday the 28th December 1878 from the Cottage Hospital where she worked. Every police officer was on duty in full uniform lining the streets as a mark of respect. I watched from Bradford Street as eighteen men in full South Staffordshire Railway uniform began walking the procession route as escort for her coffin. Sister Dora's coffin was draped in purple velvet with a design of white and gold. She had developed such a bond with the railway employees that she specifically requested them for the task. Walsall people from the richest to the most wretched turned out on that most dreary of days to mark her passing. The muffled background toll from St. Matthew's bell was the soundtrack of the day. The tearful crowd sobbed with real affection as Dora moved past them and almost every left arm adorned a black band of mourning. Then from the hospital the destination was the graveyard in Queen Street. Hundreds of locals rushed at one point towards the cemetery, some making a dangerous shortcut across the railway lines. Our brief attempt to stop them was futile and ended in failure. Numerous dignitaries attended to pay their respects including the Mayor, the Magistrates, Physicians, Ministers of Religion, Governors of Queen Mary's school, two Bishops and every one else who could get there. It was a very sad occasion, this lady had unselfishly served the towns people for well over a decade and touched so many families with her loving presence. It took almost two hours to complete the mile long route through the densely filled and partially snow covered streets. On arrival at the small cemetery chapel, four other coffins were already there from the workhouse resulting in hers remaining in the porch. The five funerals were presided over simultaneously, she was united with the people even in death. When the coffin eventually arrived at the graveside, every hat in sight was removed and the crowd parted like the waves to let her nursing

71

colleagues through. She really was a sister to every inhabitant of the town at that moment in time. In 1886, Dorothy had her statue erected on the bridge, the first statue of a working woman in the country. She also had roads, buildings, stained glass in the church and even a steam train dedicated to her memory. Her memory will remain in the hearts of many Walsall people for centuries to come.

In the spring of 1879, we were blessed with a daughter who we called Alice, a beautiful baby girl. [66] It was so awfully sad to say our goodbye's just a few weeks later, when she was torn from our arms. [67] The pain my own mother and father felt when they lost a child, was now mine, heartbreaking and indescribable! Life goes on they say and I knew that when life puts you on the ground, your only hope was to get back up. Sarah was obviously devastated but she was the bravest person I knew and hid it from the rest of us. This was another event she locked into her emotional drawer of hurt, deep inside her mind.

The Walsall market bell that I mentioned earlier, was now mine to ring! I had become on occasions, the constable charged with ringing it last thing at night. It was normally done at ten o'clock, the time for stall holders to cease trading, pack up and go home. Selling anything after that time meant they broke the Walsall market bye laws made by the council. The Mayor in charge of the council bye-laws was often also the chairman of the magistrates bench. People who got caught were always in for a roasting when they got to court. Traders came to Walsall from all around the neighbouring towns and villages to sell their wares. They obviously didn't want to haul unsold stuff and produce back with them when they left, so they usually tried their luck. You can imagine the charismatic character of some of these traders, saying, 'just going officer' and the like. Most would eventually go, with gentle persuasion, but some just refused to listen either to the bell or me.

In 1879, one such man was Alfie Wood, who I asked time and time again to pack up. He kept going and going until at ten past eleven, I reported him for failing to wrap his business up for the day. He failed or refused to appear for his summons but in his absence the magistrates fined him ten shillings and if it wasn't paid that very day he could go to prison for three weeks. I don't think they were impressed with a Brummie overstepping the mark in their town. Either way it was a hell of a message and a rap across the knuckles. [68]

In 1880 our little girl Frances was born, she was a free soul from the word go, such a strong girl who knew her own mind, wouldn't listen to a word or be told anything, but we loved her all the same. [69]

Occasionally, Walsall had some large scale disturbances in the town centre at night. There is nothing quite like a good scrap, to bring a police shift together. When these riots happened, you relied upon your mates on the shift to watch your back. The drink turned people into animals, reducing them down to the most barbaric primal functionality. One family of trouble was the Durkin's, who were originally of Irish descent. Bernard Durkin was a militiaman and self confessed hard man, an all round bad one. He was wanted by the police for violently assaulting a young girl Emily Reynolds and stealing money from her on the 3rd March 1880. Having already stolen money from her earlier that day, he returned to her house after midnight with two unknown mates. The brutish bully forced entry and he threatened to blind her with a lamp. With his hands around her throat, he robbed her of another five shillings from her pocket. Not content with his crime, he dragged her out into the backyard where he gave her a savage kicking whilst the others held her down. A nasty vicious attack on a young woman just to finance his drinking problem.

We all knew that when we came across him in the town we would have problems bringing him in. On the night of Monday the 26th April 1880, we had reports of a disturbance at a pub in Wolverhampton Street, in the Town End Bank part of the town. It turned out to be several members of the Durkin family, the mother Ann who was forty-eight, and three of her offspring, Bernard twenty-six, Mary twenty-three and John twenty. Bernard Durkin was already drunk, when he went into the pub with a couple of his militia mates. He took a drink out of an old man's hand, then almost cut his eye out when he complained. Police Constable Chandler turned up but Durkin went berserk taking off his belt to use as a weapon. A violent struggle ensued with him biting, gouging and kicking to escape. It took four officers to apprehend him, every one being assaulted in the process. Durkin then had to be carried to the police station like a madman, fighting every inch of the way. During the affray, the mother, Ann Durkin, kicked Police Constable Williams whilst he was assisting to restrain a prisoner. She then moved on to attack Police Constable Chandler, who fell to the ground. She kicked him like a wildcat, scratching and lashing out. The whole family joined the melee, with me and acting Sergeant Jackson having a right 'up and downer' with John Durkin. We both got assaulted for our efforts, he bit my arm like a rabid wild dog, drawing blood. Mary Durkin attacked Police Constable Marshall as he came to assist.

The whole family spent the night in the cells sobering up. The next morning they all climbed the stairs of shame up to the dock in the magistrates court. The mother Ann, denied assaulting any officers, but she had several previous convictions and was sent to gaol for three months with hard labour. Bernard apologised to the bench, saying he would enlist in the regular army if they were merciful. The magistrates said his behaviour was shocking and he disgraced the wearing of Her Majesty's uniform. With four previous convictions the bench gave him three months with hard labour for each of the five assaults. They insisted that the sentences would be served consecutive and not concurrent, that's fifteen months in total. John Durkin had twelve previous convictions and was given three months with hard labour. Mary Durkin had sixteen previous convictions and was ordered to pay forty shillings or have one month's imprisonment. There was no way on earth she could afford the two quid. In those days punishment was handed out swiftly and gaol was often the preferred option because the fines could not be afforded. It may not have reformed their already well moulded characters, but it prevented them from offending again for a while. [70]

In September 1880, I brought a succession of market traders to court for selling after permitted hours. There were two from Walsall, James Drew the butcher from Hall Lane and Joseph Poutney, fruit and vegetable seller, from the Square. The other three were from Birmingham, Thomas Collins and Alfred Parker selling fish and George Hicks selling fruit. When the law can't persuade them to stop it has to be enforced. The magistrates gave them all a good slap on the wrists and a financial deterrent with a one shilling fine and one guinea costs. The fines given out were as stinging as a paper cut and tended to be remembered the next time I asked them to pack up. [71] [72]

Cracks started to appear between the Reeves and the Hammond factions of our family. On one hand, I was trying to deliver law and justice to the people of Walsall and on the other, the Hammond's were fast masterminding their own criminal organisation. Our views and morals were poles apart and there was very little common ground in between. The reality was, only mother was holding us all together.

Jim Hammond married Lucy Ruff at St. Peter's Church in Walsall when he was twenty-five. The witnesses to the ceremony on the 23rd January 1881 were Frederick Bond and his wife Annie. The Ruff family were as bad as the Hammond's, this was a marriage of like minded people and the best man Bond was also notorious villain. [73]

On the 3rd January 1881, Benjamin Hammond, George Gould and another man were poaching for rabbits with a dog on land at Calderfield Farm. The land was under the control of John Myatt who challenged them with one of his labourers, James Brown. The gang physically assaulted both men and then made good their escape across the fields.

The gamekeepers shadowed them into Walsall town centre, where they vanished like magicians into thin air. Nobody knew the back alleys and the rat runs of the town better that the poachers, who were used to evading the law. After being given their names, the police soon tracked down and arrested both men. They claimed to have been casting brass at Mr. Kendrick's works and knew nothing about the rabbits. At court on the 12th February, Mr. Kendrick's foreman, Joseph Mason said he believed they were at work on the day in question. The magistrates smelt a rat and adjourned the case for two weeks so that Mr. Kendrick could attend himself. Returning to court on the 26th February, Mr. Kendrick said he was not at his place of business on the day in question. His son did inform him they were both at work, but he personally could not say for sure. Believing Myatt and Brown had made positive identifications the magistrates found both defendants guilty. Each was fined twenty shillings and costs for the trespass and ten shillings and costs for the assaults on Myatt and Brown. Those fines were far too large for them ever to have been paid. This case illustrated how the Hammonds called on witnesses to commit perjury to help them when necessary. Old man Kendrick probably took the odd bit of knock-off from them and they had him over a barrel. Despite dodgy testimony the magistrates weren't often fooled, they knew the truth when they heard it.
74 75

Children couldn't expect the courts mercy, if they got caught stealing. On the 12th February 1881, three young lads, Thomas Winter, eleven years, Thomas Elwell, eleven years and Joseph Webster, twelve years stole some caps from Frank Keeps shop in the High Street. Elwell and Webster's crimes were discovered by their parents. Their fathers issued their own parental justice, then brought them into the police station. All three boys appeared at court charged with the theft of the caps. Despite admitting their part and pleading guilty, they were all ordered to be imprisoned for three days and then to receive six strokes of corporal punishment with the birch from Detective Sergeant Drury. Theft was a serious matter and hard working shopkeepers required the court to teach them a lesson. It was believed a swift sharp shock stopped petty crime in its tracks. [76]

To round up the family in spring 1881, my mother and bricklaying step-father Ben Hammond, were living in an old courtyard house in Ablewell Street. My two half-brothers Benjamin, twenty-six and Edward nineteen, were both brass casters and lived with them. [77] I lived at Barleyfield Row, with Sarah, step-son Robert and our children, William Henry, three years and Frances who was ten months. [78] My eldest brother, William Reeves was a head boatman on the canal barges and lived in Wolverhampton Street near the cut. [79] Sarah Bullers, my sister was living in Whitehall Road with her husband Thomas and son William, both spur makers. [80] Brother Enoch Reeves was a brass caster living in Bridgman Street with his wife and daughter, both named Mary Jane. [81] Youngest brother Abel Reeves lived with his wife Emma in Birmingham Street in a courtyard house. Living with them were his two children, Thomas Benjamin, eight years and Sarah Jane, two years and his blind mother-in-law who was seventy-eight. [82] Jim Hammond, now twenty-five lived with his wife, Lucy in Newhall Street. [83]

Abel my brother, lost his wife Emma at the start of 1882, which left him a widower alone with three young children all under ten years of age. [84] The funeral was a deeply sad affair, when she died Emma was only thirty-nine years old. The poor children and their little faces were heart wrenching, we were all rocked by the unexpected grief. Abel was the youngest of the Reeves children and had never known anything other than Benjamin Hammond and our mother as his parents. This obviously made him very close to his half-brothers and they gathered around him at this time of need as did we all.

A few weeks later on the 10th April 1882, the family got together again at St. George's Church, this time for a happier occasion. My twenty-two year old step-brother, Edward Hammond got married to Annie Milner his twenty-one year old bride. [85] This wasn't a match made in heaven, the couple never seemed suited to me. There was something awkward about the match, I could not put my finger on it at the time, most likely his mother-in-law. I liked Edward, he was harmless and his elder Hammond brothers did not really include him in their business. Most probably because they thought he was too half soaked. I think he just wanted to keep out of trouble and was happy to show a bond to me to keep his distance.

I had three cases in court on the 12th April 1882, the first Archibald Sayers was fined five shillings and costs for being drunk in Intown Row or ten days in gaol with hard labour. [86] Next, Bridget Broadway refused to leave the Hare and Hounds when requested and was fined two shillings with costs or six days imprisonment. Finally, Mary Morris from Beehive Yard was found guilty for using bad language. Interestingly in court that day was Bernard Durkin, one of the notorious violent clan mentioned earlier. He sneered at me while waiting to face the magistrates for using bad language in the Barrel Inn in Margaret Street. He was only recently released from prison, but had stayed out of trouble for only a short while. His drunken crimes had been heard by the magistrates several times over the years and their patience was wearing thin. They whacked him with a fine of forty shillings knowing he would have to do the one month with hard labour instead. He fought the law, and the law won. Needless to say I had the last laugh when he was taken back down the steps.

In 1882 soon after my brother Abel's wife's untimely death, he started a relationship with a married woman named Sophia Dolphin. It was complicated because Sophia had an illegitimate daughter, Mary Jane before she married her husband William Dolphin in 1880. [87] [88] Jim Hammond was Mary Jane's natural father so she was my half-niece. [89] The young girl was often at my mothers house as she was her grandmother. Abel was a grieving widower and Sophia had just lost a son, it was a rebound relationship. Sophia abandoned her marriage with a husband who was twelve years older than her and a drunken wife beater. At the beginning of 1883, Sophia found herself pregnant with Abel's child so hatched a plan to get married again. Now for Abel it was perfectly legal, he was a widower but Sophia was still technically married to Dolphin. Working class people couldn't get divorced, the process was far too complicated and costly. Many people faced with this dilemma thought it was far better to have an illegal marriage than none at all. After all God always forgave the sins of his flock and the law had to find you out! The vicar at St. Michael's Church, Rushall was led to believe that Sophia was a spinster and her surname was Slangud. There was no such name in reality and there was no other people in the country with that name. They married on the 12th February 1883 in front of mainly family, who turned their 'blind eyes' away. [90] There was not a murmur, when the vicar asked if anyone knew of any lawful reason why they should not marry, you could have heard a pin drop. Edward Hammond and his new wife Annie were the witnesses. Her husband Dolphin was probably glad to get rid of her, they never really got on. In any case I don't think he had the guts to battle it out with the Hammond's. In 1886 Dolphin died in a sorry state and everything was soon forgotten or brushed under the carpet at any rate. [91] It put me in a difficult position, but he was my brother and they trusted me as one of their own, which of course I was. They say, blood is thicker than water, and who was it hurting? I couldn't help but think about the welfare of the children who relied on a stable family.

Love must have been in the air, half-brother Benjamin Hammond, now twenty-eight married the following week at St. George's Church on the 18th February 1883. [92] His nineteen year old bride was Matilda Ruff, half-sister of Lucy, Jim's wife. It really was a family affair in more ways than one, with Jim and Lucy Hammond being the witnesses to the proceeding. Lucy and Matilda's brother was John Ruff, a trusted member of Ben and Jim's criminal enterprise. The Hammond brothers had solemnised their relationships with the Ruff's and pooled their genetic talents to take on the law.

Chapter Seven

Twilight Trespass

There was a chasmic divide in the 1880's between those who had, and those who had not! These circumstances made poor districts and parishes a breeding ground for inventive plans to make ends meet. People pooled ideas and thoughts about how to make life easier for the families, desperate to survive. At night in their flickering candlelit rooms, fires burned and broth boiled on the grates. Their pots contained whatever was available for them to eat, but mostly poor quality, insufficient quantity and low in nutrition. The food just about kept them fed, keeping them just above the starvation level. The Hammond's didn't want to be hungry and they didn't want their children to be suffering from malnutrition. Necessity is the mother of invention, they say. In the pubs and inns the men of the Hammond family met with like minded people to plot how to keep their families fed. They knew that poor diet meant poor health and poor health meant early graves. In the darkened corners of these haunts they gathered to conspire and plan to steal from the wealthy, who had plenty and get the things honest work could not provide. The hardest thing to work out, was how to not get caught. The Hammond gang were hardened by life and sharpened by their surroundings. Having dipped their toes in the pool of crime they were now ready to dive in deep. They stole enough game to feed themselves and demand was high from the poor to have a share at the right price. If you wanted cheap meat, rabbit, pheasant, fish, ducks, geese then the Hammonds could get it. The gang was now in the early stages of becoming the most notorious law breaking family in the district with a flare for theft, violence, gambling and anything else they could think of. When the police rounded up the usual suspects, the

Hammond's were never far away from the top of their list. They were responsible for racketeering and black market dealing in the town and had organised links to various other local men of dubious character. Stolen property could vanish into the courtyards of Walsall with a little help of Hammond magic. The evidence would be consumed within hours leaving nothing for the law to find, even if they came. The local privileged landowners were seen as fair game, literally, all of their game was a fair target for the Hammond gang. Jim Hammond became the leading gangster of the organised backstreet troop. I referred to them as the 'Twilight Trawlers', as they crept out at dusk with nets trawling the fields for game, rabbits, ducks and fowl.

As time went on they became more confident and ruthless, fully prepared to fight their way out of trouble if confronted. Both police and gamekeepers alike were forced to remember encounters with them while nursing their cuts and bruises. The local poor people saw the Hammond's as their urban heroes, with Jim being their Robin Hood, helping to fill their pots with cheap meat. The gang knew that taking on the law was a risky business, especially if violence was used. The hangman's noose was just around the corner if things ever went too far. Jim Hammond laughed in the face of the law. He could always call in favours from people who had taken his quarry, by asking them to stand false witness against police prosecutions. He was always somewhere else at the time in question! Life continued, but I sensed that the Hammond's were going to make things very difficult for me in my position of authority. Our relationship became frosty at first but soon began to freeze over all together as I realised I had to put some distance between us for professional reasons.

During 1883 the magistrates continued to dish out punishments to the parishioners of Walsall. I arrested Patrick Harrison in March who was making his thirteenth appearance for drunkenness and foul language. His fine was twenty shillings, a whole pound but he took the month in gaol with hard labour instead. [93] I found Charlotte Rawson drunk on a Sunday morning near the steps of St. Matthew's church. She was fined ten shillings or two weeks in gaol. [94] I'm sure the fines were designed to remove their ability to pay for the booze but most of them were happy to do the time in prison. That's probably where the saying, 'If you can't do the time, don't do the crime' comes from.

On the 27th April 1883, Ben Hammond and his brother-in-law John Ruff, were spotted by Police Constable Kelly. They were on land at Longwood, together with another unknown man and a dog. Police Constable Kelly cautiously approached Ben Hammond who he knew was a notorious poacher. Ben decided to fight, kicking the constable and throwing him to the ground. The three then made their escape collecting the trapped rabbits as they went. All the evidence was gone by the time the officer got to his feet. Hammond and Ruff were both apprehended later but while they admitted walking across the land they denied any wrongdoing. The constable had been alone and had no witnesses to the events. Ben Hammond said the officer had threatened him with a stick and he was forced to defend himself. The magistrates fined them twenty shillings each or one month's imprisonment. Hammond got another five shillings for the assault to teach him a lesson. The truth was that Constable Kelly had to draw his staff such was the violence offered. He told me at the police station after the event that he thought Ben was a nasty piece of work capable of killing if he had to. He was right, the Hammond brothers could be ruthless if they were cornered like rats and I feared worse was to come. [95]

At three o'clock in the morning on the 18th August 1883 Police Constable Bailey was patrolling the Rushall branch canal at Great Barr. He came across Jim and Ben Hammond, John Ruff and another man Edwin Powell. They were all caught in the act of fishing with nets. Jim Hammond was stripped to the waist and was in the water, as the constable bravely approached. Powell offered the officer a bribe of taking some fish to turn a blind eye. Jim Hammond took four fish over to him, but the officer demanded their names and addresses so he could report them for summons. Ben Hammond gave the constable a false name. The officer was joined by the lock keeper who found seventeen fish in the defendants bags. At court on the 28th August 1883, Jim Hammond and John Ruff both got a huge fine of five pounds or two months imprisonment. This was based on their previous convictions and Powell got fined twenty shillings or one month in gaol. Ben Hammond failed to appear so the court issued a warrant for his arrest. The bench commended the officer for his bravery on tackling the four men alone in the dead of night. The magistrates knew the Hammonds were a dangerous gang and that anything could have happened near the water with no witnesses about. Benjamin Hammond was arrested and appeared at court on the 11th September 1883. He also got a five pound fine or two months in the gaol with hard labour. These were hefty punishments but did little to correct their behaviour. Once free it was business as usual. [96] [97]

In December 1883, I encountered a drunk named Edward Quinn who refused to go home. Despite my best efforts to reason and persuade him, I was reluctantly forced to make an arrest. He decided he wanted to fight and we got into an all out brawl. I ended up on the ground being kicked by the thug. I'm sure he wanted to kick me to death, but luckily three members of the public came to my assistance. They all got injured for their trouble, but Quinn was eventually overpowered. At court, Quinn said he had been so drunk, that he could not remember a thing about what happened. The bench took a very dim view of people assaulting the police and disorderly conduct. Drunkenness was no excuse for committing crime it was more often the cause. As a consequence the magistrates dished out sentences to match, in this case two pounds or two months with hard labour. [98]

Our daughter Rose Lilian was born in the autumn of 1883, she was our fourth child and a welcome addition to brighten our lives. [99]

Ben and Jim were released from prison, but they hadn't learnt anything from their experience. At the end of January 1884, Benjamin was back in court with John Ruff. They were charged with trespassing in the pursuit of game on land at Great Barr belonging to Mr. Bragg. At court Benjamin pleaded for the bench's mercy, but they told him promises were seldom kept by men in his position. Ben already had five convictions, so was fined twenty shillings with costs, Ruff failed to appear and was fined thirty shillings with costs. In default they both had to serve one months imprisonment. [100] [101]

At about half past ten on the night of the 23rd June 1884, the gang were back in action on private land off the Birmingham Road, Streetly. An undeterred band comprising of Benjamin Hammond, John Ruff, James Hammond and John Ireland were out to fill their bags with meat. They were completely unaware on this outing, that a reception committee was lying in wait. Sergeant Arnold had assembled a team of officers and gamekeepers supervised by William Haines, from Aston Hall. They waited patiently until they spied the poachers creeping into their fields. For fifteen minutes or more they watched them sneaking about under the hedges, setting their nets and traps. Eventually Sergeant Arnold blew his whistle signalling his men to strike against the offenders. Armed with staffs, James Hammond and John Ruff were ready to fight for freedom. As the lawmen descended upon them, they soon realised they were outnumbered and outwitted. Fighting was pointless so reluctantly they were forced to surrender. James Hammond's had a pocket full of pebbles and the others dropped theirs where they were detained. These stones would have been used as weapons of attack if the opportunity had presented itself. Numerous nets were recovered in the vicinity where the arrests were made. These were the tools of the trade for established teams of poachers.

They all appeared at Rushall Police court on the 1st July 1884, charged with trespassing for the purpose of taking game. The court was attended by Superintendent Barrett who came to view the proceedings. He had taken command of Brownhills area the previous year. To commence the proceedings, Sergeant Arnold told the court that all the defendants were well connected to numerous thieves from the Walsall area. He explained the police operation had been in response to the neighbourhood being plagued by numerous similar crimes recently. Only the previous Friday evening, two ducks had been stolen and their carcasses had been found hidden near one of the prisoners houses. The police had targeted the area in hope to apprehend the culprits, having a good idea who was responsible. Detective Sergeant Drury from Walsall Police told the court that Ruff was a well known and convicted felon. He was firmly associated with the Hammond brothers who were notorious poachers in the district.

In dramatical style, Jim Hammond protested at being called out as a thief by the sergeant. The bench then pointed out he had several convictions with his brother for poaching, a point he had to reluctantly concede to them.

All defendants claimed they had gone together for an innocent walk around Barr Beacon, denying the police allegations of poaching. Jim Hammond made a counter claim that the police and gamekeepers unnecessarily roughed him up when they were detained. He pointed the finger at Police Constable Kelly who he said prevented them from seeing their wives. He said the officer even threatened to throw his wife into a duck pond. Constable Kelly explained to the court that whilst escorting the prisoners to the railway station, several women and children had surrounded him in a menacing manner. They attempted to intimidate him with their threatening demeanour forcing him to use strong words to get past them. The officer had not forgotten the last time he ended up in a fight with Ben Hammond, so there was no love lost. Ireland protested by saying he had only ever been convicted of "that water geese job," which didn't help his cause. The bench clearly saw through their charades and found them all guilty as charged. Ireland was sentenced to one month's imprisonment with hard labour, and the others were imprisonment for two months with hard labour.

Both brothers found themselves languishing in Stafford gaol with strong suspicions that they had been grassed up by some coppers nark. They swore to find the guilty party and to get revenge, but they had nothing to go on. I would have been the most obvious suspect, but they didn't think it was me because they never talked business or said anything in my presence. In fact they had decided to freeze me out all together leaving only mother as our contact and mediator. [102] [103]

Drama was a never ending feature of this family, while Ben Hammond was away in Stafford Prison, his wife Matilda became pregnant. This was the first thing in a chain of events leading to tragedy touching the family's history yet again. What happened and why is open to speculation, but the foundations of mothers world were rocked by it all.

On Saturday the 9th August 1884, Ben was painting as part of his hard labour at the prison near some laburnum trees. Ben was twenty-nine years of age, so no kid at the time. For reasons only known to him, he ate a large quantity of deadly poisonous laburnum seeds filling his stomach. Not too long afterwards, he fell ill with severe stomach pains, causing chronic pain and diarrhoea. At first the warders thought he was trying it on, but nonetheless they transferred him to the hospital wing. The prison surgeon was called to assess his condition but by three o'clock that day he was dead. [104] [105] Ben was a switched on man, so he would have known the consequences of eating the seeds. Something must have pushed him over the cliff of human endurance, forcing him to make the decision that life just wasn't worth living anymore. There was no way anyone in that prison could have bullied or frightened him, he was just too tough for that. My guess is that he found out about Matilda and it all weighed too heavy on his mind in that solitary cell. The coroners court established that he died of poisoning as a direct result of consuming the laburnum seeds found present in his stomach. Most thought that if Ben knew about the baby, he would have rather killed the suspect than die himself. Suicide was considered the cowards way out, not something you would associate with Ben. They used to say that suicide never ends the pain, it only passes it to someone else!

There was all kind of talk about accidents, suicide, cover-ups and even murder. The truth is we will never know for sure, it will remain a mystery. Jim was racked with revenge for whoever dobbed them in for the poaching and swore that he would avenge his brothers death, an eye for an eye. The brothers were very close and it did hit Jim hard, he wanted desperately to find the person for signing Ben's death warrant. The rest of the family were traumatised, but Jim really did feel the stinging pain of bereavement. Mother was deeply affected and suffered terribly from the loss. She was mad at Ben and felt disappointed with Jim. Despite this she would always defend her boys and would have killed those responsible for what happened.

Matilda gave birth to a son, Edward James Hammond who was born on the 5th April 1885. [106] This means his conception was in July 1884 when Benjamin Hammond was still in prison. It's easy to judge or come to the wrong conclusion about these events. I knew from my police work that young women left alone with kids soon became desperate for money. Sometimes this forced them to make bad decisions, just to keep the roof over their head. I'm not saying this was the case, but unscrupulous employers and landlords sometimes offered work or shelter at a price! It can't be easy when your family and financial world fall apart by having a husband imprisoned. Sometimes the world can be a very cruel and inhospitable place in the mind of an individual. A moment of weakness can bring about the worst of decisions resulting in terrible consequences. What happened to Ben shows this, I think he probably felt the guilt of having left her at home alone and blamed himself, we may never know!

I came across women all the time in my policing career, who had fallen on hard times. One of these was Caroline James who was homeless and destitute after being thrown out on the streets by her family. The fact was at her most vulnerable, she took solace in drink and in October 1884 I found her drunk in Portland Street. I could see her predicament and tried to talk to her. It was impossible to get through to her, she was so drunk. To save her from herself, I was forced to arrest her. I could see the drink had taken a firm hold and was most likely the cause for her homelessness. It's just a pity she had no help and now the system would punish her further. It was the cruel way of the world. [107]

The constant and unrelenting family stresses and strains were having a severe and adverse effect on my mothers health. She worried and mithered about us all, but I think she realised that trying to control the activities of her Hammond sons was now beyond her. The tragic death of Ben in prison had hammered a large nail in her coffin and played a heavy part in the deterioration of her health. My sister sent word that she was in a bad way and had begun to fail fast. On the 15th November 1884, I went to be with my mother knowing she had little time left. I could see straight away that all the hassle had chased away her desire for life. She had lost any fight and her body was lifeless and her voice soft and low. I held her hand whilst looking into her eyes, I had always been her favourite, the responsible one with common sense. She never told me so in words, just in her own silent way. She knew she could trust me to do the right thing at the right time. She spoke as only a mother could, "Look after things for me". Soon after and in a totally silent and calm way her work here was done. She lifted the anchor of life and drifted away into her eternity. [108] The cause of her death was

89

certified as 'old age' by the surgeon, William Oliver. Hard stressful years had ploughed deep wrinkles into her face, but she was only just sixty-four, not really old at all. Inside I was broken, as if something had been surgically removed leaving a void impossible to refill. I could not help but lay the blame on the two Hammond boys for her demise. This day was the cut off, the line in the sand with their shenanigans. Between them they had put my mother in an early grave. Ben took the easy way out when the going got tough, leaving all his problems for someone else to sort out. Mother tried to shoulder the weight of his death but the pressure proved too hard to bare. She had closely followed him to the next world, creating a huge crater in the Reeves family structure.

I was generally the person in the family who had to mop up the mess created by others, the things other people didn't fancy doing. It was me who sorted mums affairs out and kept the ship afloat long enough to see her go to her final resting place. Jim was still grieving Ben's passing when mother died and he was obsessed with finding the person who grassed them up. He now had lost his mother and was very volatile and totally unreliable. I think every family has woodlice who crawl back into the woodwork when something needs doing. I was nearly always on my own when family tragedy struck.

As time went by, I heard never ending rumours that Jim thought I might have had something to do with his arrest. He was so deep in his own grief and life, he was blind to everyone else's problems. He never thought for one minute, that his and Ben's gaol terms hurt mother and made her life shorter. It was all about him, he never had the nerve to front me directly even though I expected it would come.

I thought there might be some trouble at mothers funeral with Jim and his cronies. I convinced Sarah, my wife who was heavily pregnant to stay at home when mother was buried. I sold it to her because I didn't want her distressed because of the baby and our previous problems. The reality was I knew that if Jim wanted to cause trouble with me, I was never going to back down. If he dared to be disrespectful at mother's funeral, I was going to teach him a lesson once and for all. Mother could not protect him this time if he wanted to settle the matter. It took a lot for me to lose my cool, but once I had, it was an ugly sight and I could not afford for Sarah to watch the spectacle. She knew only too well what happened to men who lost their tempers and she did not need reminding. Things seen cannot be unseen and nobody knew that better than me.

When the day came, there were lots of strained views between us all, mainly Jim towards me. I think he was watching for some sign of guilt from me, before he made his move. I had brothers, Bill and Enoch at my side and sister Sarah and her husband in support, Abel was pretty much in the centre and young Eddie Hammond looked up to me and didn't want to get involved in any trouble. At the end of the day, Jim realised I was not going to take any nonsense from him. At least for the time being, he decided that discretion was the better part of valour and wound his neck in. Mum had been the glue that held the family together and with her gone so were the ties between the Reeves's and Hammond's. In that, I really mean Jim and me, you could cut the tension between us with a knife. After the funeral I had very little to do with Jim, but to be fair I had plenty of other family things to focus on. Early in 1885, me and Sarah had another son, George Thomas. [109]

The winter of 1885 was extremely cold with snow falling every month from October all the way through into spring. Things were incredibly difficult at home, with four children and now twins on the way.

Scrapping and drunkenness carried on in March when Thomas Simmons got into a fight with Harry Oswin, the landlord of the New Tavern in Stafford Street. The landlord refused to serve him because he was so drunk then he tore a sleeve off Harry's coat. He was still trying his best to get into the pub when I arrived. I reported him but he failed to turn up at court so was fined twenty-one shillings or twenty-one days in gaol. [110]

Sometimes in life when things get hard, you are tested to the end of your tether. Mother used to say, you need the 'Patience of Job,' to get through life. The year of 1886 was a annus horribilis for me and Sarah. In autumn our little boy George Thomas died, just one year old. [111] This rocked us both, but Sarah was pregnant with the twins. To see her so upset almost broke my heart and I feared the worst. This was a hard blow to the solar plexus, bringing us both down to our knees and testing our very faith and resolve. Just a few months later the twins, Gertrude and Laura Louisa were born lifting us out of the mire. [112] [113] With only one foot out of our trench of pain following George's death, we were kicked in the head, falling face down back into the bitterest turmoil. Gertrude was to die shortly after her birth and Laura Louisa fell asleep with her twin sister early in the New year. [114] [115] Of the seven children we had been blessed with, just three were alive. It felt like an unbearable curse had befallen us taking away our light with its cloak of death. We should have been broken by it all, but we clung to each other with white knuckles weathering the emotional storm and hanging on for dear life! There were times that it would have been far easier to let go, but we held on stronger for the little ones who needed us so much.

In the summer of 1886, I was appointed as deputy-inspector in charge of the police weights and measures department. [116] This was technically a promotion and involved me taking on a lot of extra responsibility. Most things sold by traders had to be bought using the correct unit of measurement, whether it be product weight or fluid measure. Vegetables, meat, beer, milk, flour, bread, spirits, oil, other foods, coal, every material had to be weighed and measured. The law stipulated that certain weights and measures had to be stamped by the Weights and Measures Office to confirm they were correct. This was to protect the public from being given short measures by unscrupulous sellers. Law enforcement was seen as essential to stop the fiddling. At least these laws had the support of the public who despised being short changed.

The fact was there were plenty of dodgy dealing going on in the town. In September 1886, I prosecuted two local coal dealers, Kate Taylor from Dudley Street and James Williams of Milton Street who were fined for having unjust weights. [117]

Unexpectedly Bill, my elder brother died at the end of 1887, he was just fifty years of age. [118] He never married or had children and lived all his life as a boatman on the canals. His life seemed to come and go without hardly leaving a trace on the world in which we live. Apart from us siblings, he had no family. We rarely saw him as he spent his life hauling loads around the Birmingham Canal network. It makes you wonder what life is all about, was he born just to be a beast of burden with not even the blessing of children?

My new job meant my patch was the whole borough of Walsall and I was left to almost supervise myself so long as I got the results. To be fair the public were always ready to report dodgy measures, so I didn't have to search too hard. This was the case with Samson Dawson who had a grocery shop in High Street, Bloxwich. [119] I found his scales were six drams against the purchaser and he was fined twenty shillings and costs. He was reprimanded to the effect that he could have been fined five pounds so he could consider himself lucky.

In the town of Walsall, there was an undefined base class of people living without morals or care. These almost ferrel people were unrefined, uneducated and dragged up in a world of gloom, without prospect or expectation. Poverty and hunger kept them in their place, nothing to do with gender or race. It's no wonder with everything stacked against them that they turned out that way. At least fifty percent of these people were women. To them, course and obscene language was a way of life and part of their everyday vocabulary. Nothing was better at demonstrating this than a drunken woman late at night. In May 1887, Ellen Henry was ejected by the landlady from the Nelson and Peal public house in Peal Street. She used the most obscene language you could possibly imagine spilling from the lips of a woman. When I turned up and politely asked her to go home, I received a barrage of obscenities. After a few attempts to get her to go home, she finally persuaded me that to arrest her was the only way forward. It turned into a very expensive night out for her. She was fined five shillings or fourteen days in gaol for her trouble. [120]

In July 1887, a twenty year old Elizabeth Burke was out of her tree drunk as a skunk in Hill Street. She bellowed out a string of disgusting language at the top of her voice, but refused to listen to a word I said. Upon arrest she transformed into a tigress, ripping all the buttons from my coat. I literally dragged her to the cells. The next day the court slapped her with a five shillings fine or ten days in gaol. [121]

The very same month, I arrested Lucy Meacham and Mary Flood for being drunk and disorderly and using bad language. They were both from Wisemore, which was a pretty rough area in those days. Foolishly they joked about their behaviour and clowned about in court in front of the bench. You may have heard the saying, 'when you are in a hole stop digging,' but I don't think they knew those wise words. The magistrates wiped the smile right off their faces by sending them both to gaol for twenty-one days even though they pleaded guilty. [122]

The hard work I did as assistant inspector of weights and measures was being recognised much to my delight. Representations were made to the Watch Committee in August 1887, who in turn rewarded me with a pay rise of an extra one shilling and sixpence per week. [123] At the time the force was commanded by acting Chief Constable Drury, following the resignation of Mr. Tewsley who moved to the Reading force as their new chief constable. Drury was the forces detective sergeant and always stood up for his men, commanding everyones respect.

I continued investigating none compliance with the legislation, like John Freeman the sweet shop owner in Marsh Street. He had unstamped weights costing him a shillings fine and ten shillings and sixpence costs. [124]

In between this work drunks continued to roll in, like James Leonard of Dudley Street in April 1888, who had seven previous convictions and was fined ten shillings or twenty-one days. [125] In May 1888, I locked up Micky Mitchell from Bull's Head Yard. He begged the bench to be merciful but they were having none of it. He had appeared before them eleven times previously and was fined ten shillings or fourteen days in the cells. [126]

On the 14th May 1888, Jim Hammond appeared at Rushall Police Court having been apprehended on George Bragg's land at Great Barr again. He was found trespassing in Blackwoods, Great Barr with Frank Coleman and James Morgan looking for game with dogs. When the gamekeepers moved in they were stoned by the poachers. They were all fined twenty shillings or one months imprisonment. [127]

If there was one thing Walsall people hated, it was being ripped off and being given short measures. Money was hard to come by and I was getting information from all sorts of aggrieved people. Someone tipped me off about Richard Horton the grocer in Lower Rushall Street. They told me his weights were suspect, so I visited him and found two of his weights under measure. He told the magistrates that he had only been in the town a short time and he got the weights when he bought the shop. They still fined him five shillings and costs. [128]

I was earning my pay award ten times over to the joy of the magistrates and my bosses. Even the locals were glad to see the shop keepers prosecuted as they could have been fiddling them for years. It was a win win situation, only the shopkeepers were bearing the cost, but to be honest it was their own fault. In June 1888, I brought two local licensees to court. The first, Eddie Ingram from the Shinglers Arms in Green Lane, who had unstamped weights. I had asked him to get them done previously but he said the office was closed when he went. As the weights were actually correct he was just ordered to pay the costs. Secondly, Joseph Haynes from the Irish Harp in Long Street, also for unstamped measures. I had reprimanded him about the matter six months previously, but he had completely ignored the warning. The magistrates fined him twenty shillings and costs and confiscated his measures. [129] [130] He might think twice before ignoring my visits again!

Towards the end of August 1888, me and Sarah had a son, Enoch Edward, who became a fine addition to the family and we were overjoyed at the blessing. [131] We prayed that he be allowed to grow into adulthood. It was always a lottery, there never seemed any reason why some children made it and others did not. People used to say that God chose his little angels for himself.

I never liked deceitful people, but Thomas Glover who owned the sweet shop in Blue Lane West, was certainly one of them. His shop was probably the biggest in the whole town. I visited and found that one of his two ounce weights was under measure and this was the one he used all the time to fiddle the poor families. He was a conceited man and told me I couldn't do anything to stop him making his business pay. In January 1889, he told the court that he was a very poor man only making a shilling a week. Gaining the pity of the magistrates they fined him five shillings. Hearing this result he turned to me and smiled. This was a bad move by him, I immediately protested to them that he was lying and in fact he had the biggest shop of its type in the whole borough. They were furious with his attempt to mislead the court and fined him ten shillings and he had to forfeit his weight's. I also made it my business to let the locals know they were being ripped off by him and before long he really was the poor man he talked about. [132]

On the 25th October 1889, Inspector Robert Drury retired from the force after thirty-two years service. A meeting was held at the guildhall to present him with a portrait commissioned by members of the force as a retirement gift. The meeting was marked by the attendance of numerous important members of the council, including the mayor and Mr. Taylor the chief constable. It was quite an emotional scene to see him retire with so much respect from all those distinguished men who attended. He had always been a friend and had helped me get a pay rise to help my family. Although he was an inspector he was basically the top man in all but name and well respected by all of his colleagues. [133]

In November 1889, I visited Edward Morris the miller in Stafford Street. He had two fifty-six pound weights, both were under measure. His solicitor said he bought the weights at a sale and the weights were not being used. Despite his attempts to get mercy from the magistrates they fined him forty shillings. [134]

At the end of 1889 my sixty-five year old step-father Benjamin Hammond passed away. [135] The funeral went off without issue, apart from acknowledging each other, I did not speak with Jim. I suppose now that our parents were gone, there was no need for us to pretend that we were brothers. We both mutually wanted to get on with our lives without interference from each other.

All work and no play, slowly started to take its toll on me and by January 1890, my health had taken a turn for the worse. I struggled with the new workload combined with the rigours of family life. My health concerns were reported by the Watch Committee of the council such was the good work I did. [136] I'm guessing, life had just caught up with me, forcing me to stop. My brain was overloaded with hundreds of random thoughts and worries and I could not think straight. I basically needed a rest, everybody else's problems had now been transferred to me. I had become depressed and in a world of personal turmoil, I just could not see the wood for the trees. I think I must have just taken on too many woes of the world. Sarah was always at my side and I had to pull myself together for hers and the children's sake. Like I said before, I was in a hole, I had to stop digging and work out how to climb out of it.

Just to show how diverse my police role was, in April 1889, I prosecuted four cases of selling bread that had not been weighed. The cases under the Bread Act of 1836 were brought by the Chief Constable against Herbert Starkey, High Street, Bloxwich; Samuel Cooper, Reeves Street, Bloxwich; Phoebe Wilkinson, Elmore Row, Bloxwich and Henry Webb, grocer, Oxford Street, Pleck. In fact, these were the first cases ever brought under this act in the town. Test cases for the magistrates to deliberate over. The Chief Constable addressed the bench by saying he knew a fine of forty shillings could be imposed. He personally wanted these cases to send a message to all sellers, that bread had to be weighed and that bakers who went around in carts were required to carry scales. Each defendant received a fine of five shillings with costs. [137]

On the 21st February 1890, Matilda, Benjamin Hammond's widow married Robert Jones at St. George's Church. [138] They both lived in Bott Lane, with Matilda's three children, the youngest two being illegitimate.

John Wyatt Cater my old chief constable died on the 9th March 1890. [139] He had served the town police for thirty-one years and was greatly respected by all the officers and townsfolk alike. Walsall Police Force turned out in almost its entirety to attend his funeral at St. Michael's Church, Rushall on Friday the 14th March. At the age of sixty-eight, he had not been in the best of health before his death. At the churchyard, two rows of officers lined the path to the church door. His coffin was carried on the shoulders of three inspectors, a sergeant and two constables. Several of the local dignitaries attended the service as a mark of their utmost respect. He was a good man, the man who interviewed and offered me the job in policing.

In late April 1890, our son Arthur Ernest was born, he was to become inseparable from his brother Enoch. [140] He was a good strong lad and I felt sure he would survive the trepidations of infancy, God willing. The two of them reminded me of the relationship I had with my younger brother Enoch.

My own relationship with my brother Enoch was to suffer a case of parting in 1890. He finally decided to leave Walsall, taking his skills as a craftsman in brass and German silver casting to America, the land of opportunity. There was nothing to keep him in Walsall and the promise of a new life had swayed his mind to go and give it a whirl. He saved enough money for himself, his wife and daughter's passage and booked the travel. After one last get together between our families he was set. I was very sad to see him go and for the first time realised how he must have felt, when I ran off to join the army, leaving him behind. He waved goodbye and off he went, emigrating to the United States where he settled in Salt Lake City, Utah. It was his time for adventure and I wished him well with a big lump in my throat. Secretly, I wished I was going with him, I had been in Walsall for the longest period in my life and although my friends and family were here my feet were getting itchy again. I realised that nothing good happened in this town only heartache.

In January of 1891, I was tipped off about James Grant from Forster Street fiddling the weights of carts collected from Old Fishley Colliery. I stopped him on the road and asked him to take two carts back to the town weighbridge for checking. He became very abusive and I eventually charged him with obstruction for failing the attitude test. I was with the Chief Constable and he was insistent that the carts were reweighed. We were right, both carts were discovered to have discrepancies in their load weights. At court we informed the magistrates that the obstruction need not be pursued and Grant conceded that he was liable for the offences under the new Weights and

Measures Act 1889. Grant's solicitor asked for leniency as this was a new law, but his scam cost him a fine of ten pounds. He was also reminded by the court that they could have fined him twenty-five pounds. I'm sure their fine accounted for the obstruction as well just to teach him a lesson. [141] [142] [143]

The time comes in every mans life when he realises the aspirations of the mind and the capabilities of the body drift apart. My body could no longer keep up with the demands of my brain. After great consideration and after some periods of severe illness, I retired from Walsall Borough Police on the 18th March 1891. [144] I wished that I could have carried on, but my time had come, after serving the good people of Walsall for the last eighteen years. Together with my military service with the 99th Regiment of thirteen and a half years, I had served the public for thirty-one years. I received a pension from the police of thirty-one pound a year and at forty-eight years old, I was determined to enjoy some of it. When I left Walsall Borough Police, the force consisted of a chief constable, thirteen sergeants and thirty-five constables. Two sergeants were detectives, one sergeant was the chief constable's clerk, one was markets inspector with another in charge of Bloxwich.

Chapter Eight

The Will to Live

On reflection times had changed quite dramatically over the ten years leading up to April 1891. The new family map looked something like this! I was living with Sarah and the family in Arundel Street, Walsall. With us lived: my step-son Robert Stanton who was a fifteen year old brush maker; son, William Henry, who was thirteen and a chemists assistant; daughter, Frances, who was ten; daughter, Rose Lillian, who was seven; and sons, Enoch Edward, who was two and Arthur Ernest, who was eleven months. [145] My sister, Sarah Bullers lived with her husband, Thomas in Newhall Street.[146] Her son, William Bullers lived in the same street with his wife and daughter. [147] Enoch Reeves was settled in Salt Lake City, Utah. Abel Reeves my youngest brother lived in a courtyard house in New Street, together with his wife Sophia. They had his three children by his first wife, Thomas, Sarah and Margaret and his wife's daughter Mary Jane. Also present were their four children, John Thomas, Abel, William and Enoch. That's eight children between seventeen and two months and they even had a lodger with only three rooms between them all! [148] Ben Hammond's widow Matilda lived in Bank Street with her new husband Robert Jones and her three children, Eliza Margaret, who was eight Edward James, who was six and Richard Thomas, aged one. [149] Jim Hammond was living in Bank Street with his wife Lucy and their four children, Eliza, Thomas, Enoch and Edward. [150] Edward Hammond was living in Bott Lane with his wife Annie, they did not have any children. [151]

After I had retired from the police, I was out for a walk on a nice summers night in July 1891. As I strolled through the town, I heard a commotion and saw a man was fighting with a former colleague, Police-constable Williams. I remembered how I needed help from the public on occasion and gratefully received it when it came. John Kelly from Gorton's Yard, was drunk and using foul language when he was arrested. He became very violent and was going mad. I had to help my old friend and went to his aid. I ended up being assaulted for my trouble, but I knew it was the right thing to do. Apparently he caused a load of damage to windows at the police station afterwards. With twenty-three previous convictions, he was sent to gaol for two months with hard labour. [152] [153]

In January 1892 we had our youngest and final son, David Sidney. [154] That meant we had six children living with us. My days of working for a living were far from over, with all those mouths to feed. I got a nice little job as watchman at the iron works and a few casual hours labouring for a bricklayer. With my pension, I was earning a decent wage and was reasonably comfortable. I was even able, for the first time to put a bit away for a rainy day. The chief constable, Christopher Taylor was always asking me to come back, but I knew that ship had sailed. [155] [156] [157] I should have been flattered, but I didn't need the hassle. I noticed at some point that my hair colour had started fading away. I still had a young family to take care of as I approached the momentous age of fifty.

In the first week of January 1894, Sarah and I were blessed with another daughter Ada Edith. [158] She was baptised at St. Paul's Church on the 26th January. Joy again turned to bitter pain only a few days later, when she sadly slipped away. [159] [160] At this time we were living in a house at 81 Queen Street, by the cemetery so we were constantly reminded of death.

You will remember, I told you the story about Abel's second wife Sophia who married him bigamously. She had a daughter, Mary Jane Stanger who was the natural daughter of Jim Hammond. Mary Jane turned out to be a chip of the old block. At the age of seventeen she ran off with her boyfriend Ernest Husted also seventeen. He had a previous conviction for shop breaking from the 11th December 1893 in Walsall. Together with another couple, Benjamin Watts, nineteen and Clara Keeling, seventeen they went off into the countryside of Worcestershire.

On the 16th September 1894, they broke into the house of Joseph Dallow stealing money and property in the parish of Acton Beachamp. Two days later they broke into another house in the parish of Bransford, belonging to George Charles. This time they stole clothing food and a watch chain. After their mini crime spree they returned to Walsall but were arrested on the 21st September for both offences of housebreaking. They all appeared at the County Magistrates Clerk's Office in Worcester on the 22nd September for breaking into the two cottages. They were remanded in custody until the following Wednesday. On that occasion they were all committed for trial. The trial took place on the 15th October 1894 at the Worcester Quarter Sessions. They were all found guilty of both housebreaking offences. Stanger, Husted and Keeling were sentenced to three months imprisonment with hard labour. Watts who was older and also with a previous conviction of two months, received six months imprisonment with hard labour. I am sure Mary Jane made both her parents proud. [161] [162] [163] [164] [165]

We still lived in Queen Street when our last and youngest child Annie was born on the 31st January 1895. [166]

I kept a bit of distance between me and Jim after his dad's funeral. I was aware his nefarious activities were still a big part of his life and if anything, he was up scaling his operations. He was a wily old fox, a proper rogue, never out of the sights of the local police, but despite this he rarely got caught for the things he was doing.

On the 3rd June 1895, my step-son Robert Stanton married Susan Thorpe at St. John's Church, Pleck and they got a house in Checkett Street. [167] [168] Robert always considered me to be his father and we were very close. He had never known anything different and never spoke about his real father, the murderer. Most likely out of the respect he had for me, but he knew it was a painful memory to his mother. He always considered himself to be one of the Reeves family and so did I, in all but name he was my son.

On the 22nd June 1896, Jim Hammond was back on Bragg's land at Great Barr. This was the land he had been caught on with Ben, before his imprisonment leading to his death. This didn't seem to deter him going back there at one o'clock in the morning, with his gang of eight men. The gamekeeper Josiah Fisher was with his son William, when they unfortunately stumbled across the Hammond gang on their land at Bourne Vale. Josiah Fisher kept watch as the poachers set their game nets all around his field. Josiah had known Jim Hammond for years and eventually shouted out to him by name. He got no reply so began to cautiously approach, knowing of their potential for violence. Five yards from the group, he was pelted with a storm of stones. In the downpour from the darkness, William Fisher's leg was so badly hurt, they were forced to retreat for their own lives. That morning, Josiah Fisher went to Jim Hammond's house with Sergeant Riley and officers from Walsall police. They all knew Jim could be a handful if he wasn't outnumbered. Sergeant Riley knocked the door and the Fishers stayed out of view, so as not to antagonise Jim before they were let in. He asked what they wanted from the upstairs window and was told to come down so they could have a word. When Jim opened the door the two Fisher's, appeared from hiding in the yard and went in to identify him. Jim's boots were wet and covered in seeds from the fields, something noticed by the police. Jim Hammond was charged with night poaching with violence.

He appeared at Rushall Police Court on the 29th June 1896, where on the day the case was reduced to night poaching only. The violence was dropped so that the court had jurisdiction to dispose of it that day.

104

This was with the consent of the police but after submissions made by Hammond's solicitor. Jim's solicitor, Mr. Jackson appeared to defend him and argued that the laws on poaching were very precise. He argued to the court that a defendant had to be found in possession of poaching instruments, nets, pegs or game to be found guilty. That being the law, Jim Hammond had not been found with any of those things so had no case to answer. The court asked if stones could be considered as such instruments, but Mr. Jackson said the law made no mention of stones at all. He said that his client was at home in bed drunk from the previous night when the offence took place. He claimed that this was simply a case of mistaken identity. A witness Ellen Bates was called to say, her husband had been out drinking with Hammond all night. She said that at about eleven-thirty, she had helped Jim Hammond's wife get her blind drunk husband up stairs to bed. Reluctantly the bench acquitted Hammond, conceding that the case had not been made out, due to the lack of poaching implements in his possession. On letting him free from court the Bench said they were convinced Hammond was responsible and was there at the time. [169] [170] [171] [172]

Both the court and the police were unhappy with the outcome and the sense that justice had not been served. A clandestine meeting between the police and magistrates took place afterwards behind closed doors, they desperately needed justice to be done. They could not allow people like Jim Hammond to exploit loopholes in the law and ridicule the judicial system. A plan was hatched to bring him back to court again. On the 13th July, Jim found himself back in court at Rushall charged this time, with assaulting William Fisher, under gamekeeper at Great Barr on the 22nd June 1896. They had decided to have another 'bite at the cherry', by resurrecting the assault even though they all agreed to drop it first time around. They really did want to get Jim, he was a thorn in their side and a menace to the local landowners who were friends to members of the bench. Mr. Jackson, his solicitor complained that the charge of assault should not have been brought against him following his acquittal, as it was an abuse of process against his client. His submission was over-ruled and the evidence of William Fisher's assault on the night in question was heard again. Neither, Mr. Jackson's contempt for the prosecution's validity, nor Hammond's not guilty plea prevented them convicting him of the assault. It all looked like the result of a done deal, cut and dried before they started. He was fined ten shillings with thirteen shillings costs or fourteen days in prison. The law had been pliably moulded around the facts of the case to convict him, which only goes to show that you can't beat the system. You might get away with some things, some of the time, but not all things all of the time! Jim's card had been well and truly marked.

Early in 1899, the wind of tragedy was about to blow a hurricane through the Reeves household, changing our lives for ever. Any happiness was to turn to bite me like a rabid dog, when my beautiful lifelong companion became very ill. Sarah had been afflicted by the friendless tuberculosis and the fire in her heart, gradually began to flicker in its wind. As I sat at Sarah's bedside on the 7th February, I sensed the final moments were approaching as the doctor left for the last time shaking his head. The injustice was, she was still a young woman only forty-one. Years of stress and struggle had slowly whittled away her ability to fight anymore. Sarah desperately wanted to stay with us, but sank into the painful realisation that the ground beneath her feet would soon be piled on top of her head. With a knowing last glance and a few final shallow breaths, she could breathe no more. I held her hand tightly as she drifted away from me into the afterlife. [173] At that point I knew I had just two choices left, to carry on with life or die with her. I lived with duty all my life and knew I owed it to my family to paint on a brave face and carry on. When her body left our house for the final time on the day of her funeral, inwardly I grieved like never before. Every sentence ends with a full stop, my teacher used to say, how right they were. Our children were victims of the cruelest robbery, that of their mother, little Annie was four the following month and far too young to be left with just a father. At fifty-six, I was on my own again, a position I never envisaged being in, but one I had to reluctantly accept. Jim said nothing at Sarah's funeral, everyone could see how raw things were and how the kids were distraught. Not even Jim could lower himself to be that insensitive, in fact he saw the pain and I'm sure he felt it too. It's quite strange how grief can unite even the most diverse characters. To be honest Jim, with all his faults was still family and I'm sure he felt mothers presence watching his every move that day.

Jim never stopped trying to beat the system though, it was written into his character. He knew that every policeman, gamekeeper and magistrate in the area wanted him in prison, but his contempt was written in stone for it all. Jim was the figurehead in the borough for crime and disorder and you could associate him personally to every villain for miles around.

In September 1899 the chief constable personally appeared to object to the renewal of a justices licence for Edwin Roper who ran the Red House pub on Sutton Road. Thieves and villains from right across the whole Walsall Borough and beyond frequented this hostelry. Roper had no convictions himself, but his two sons had previous for poaching and assaulting Lady Scott's gamekeepers at Great Barr Hall. The chief constable decided to prosecute the case himself, because of possible witness intimidation from thugs of the criminal fraternity. Roper employed the services of Mr. Plumtre from Jackson's solicitors of Walsall who usually represented the Hammond's. The chief constable called his first witness in support of his case, a farmer by the name of Thomas Downes. He worked at Wood End Farm, which occupied adjacent land to the Red House. When Mr. Downes walked into court he noticed, Jim Hammond and his brother-in-law John Ruff, sitting in the public area. He knew them both to be notorious villains out of the back streets of Walsall. He was in an impossible position, between the devil and the deep blue sea. He knew that if he spoke out, he would never get them off his back. Whatever the police said, in reality they were powerless to protect him. He knew that he had to keep his mouth shut and become a hostile witness. Greatly to the annoyance of the chief constable, he repeatedly failed to give any answers in support of the police case. He was asked outright if he felt intimated, but still refused to comment and the proceedings started grinding to a standstill. The frustrated magistrates sensed something odd was going on. They witnessed the glances between Downes and Hammond taking place after each question was asked. In the end they ordered all the witnesses to wait outside. Hammond, Ruff and a few others showed their contempt by breaking out into fits of laughter, as they were ushered out. The chief constable then called John Ruff to interrogate him about how many times he frequented the Red House. He wanted to highlight to the court that convicted villains frequented the place regularly. Ruff was not going to make things easy for him by saying he only called when he had 'a spare ha'pence'. This amused the courts audience who broke into laughter again. The chief constable was noticeably annoyed and losing his patience with the proceedings. He outright demanded Ruff to declare if he was a convicted poacher. Mr. Plumtre, Ruff's solicitor intervened and told him not to answer the question further frustrating him. He then made a submission that the chief constable was not acting correctly in accordance with court etiquette. After deliberating, the bench decided to ask Ruff themselves if he was a convicted felon. With Mr. Plumtre's permission, he confirmed that he had served a total of seven years in prison. The chief constable quickly followed up, alleging that Ruff had recently been fined forty shillings at court. Ruff mockingly said the chief constable had got his facts wrong. The bench looked at each other in confusion. Ruff then said, he had refused to pay the fine and instead did ten days in prison. His attempt to humiliate the police chief resulted in more cries of laughter. Jim Hammond was next to come into court, to further the comedy show. When asked, he said he visited the Red House about once a month. The last time being last Saturday, which was the first time in a month. He explained that whenever he travelled that way, he benefited by getting half-a-pint of ale at Roper's. It was like a standup comedy act, again reducing the court to laughter. Hammond told the court the chief constable had no right to misrepresent him up and down the country as a villain, when he had only ever been guilty of a "disdemeanour". To correct him they asked, if he meant, misdemeanour. He replied, "You can miss it how you like," bringing tears to the eyes of his audience. Sergeant Riley was summoned into court to read out Hammond's previous convictions. After the sergeant finished, Jim duly refused to accept the convictions were either true or his. Mr. Plumtre told the court that the chief constable's case for objecting to the licence was weak. He told the bench the pub had been in the Roper family's possession for sixty years and there had only been one conviction for permitting drunkenness in all that time. The case was adjourned but Roper was told to find a suitable tenant for his public house. [174]

I never liked New Year for some reason, there was rarely anything to celebrate and this year was no different. With Sarah missing there was nothing I could think of to celebrate. Even the emergence of a new century could not lift my mood above my grief. The old town of Walsall was changing fast and becoming a very different place. As we moved into the twentieth century, the truth was, nothing seemed the same without Sarah, I felt so alone. Everyone seemed to be moving on with their lives and I felt trapped once again. I wondered if I was being left behind by the world, whether my adventures were over and this was my lot. My brother Enoch was living a very different life with his wife, Mary Jane and his children in Meredith Avenue, Salt Lake City. [175] He had written many times and said he would love me to visit him there. I

109

have to say the thought of moving on was very appealing. The sound of people celebrating bringing in the new year, the new century, reverberated outside, but my thoughts were all melancholy. There was no tall dark man to walk through my house with a piece of coal. There was no bringing of good luck, or any renditions of "Auld Lang Syne".

Soon after new year, William Henry my eldest son, told me he too was tired of Walsall. He suffered terribly from the loss of his mother and needed a change and had decided to join the army. What could I say, I had always spoken about how I missed military life and now he wanted a piece of it. On the 3rd February 1900, William Henry enlisted with the South Staffordshire Regiment and by March was serving with them in South Africa. At least he had broken away from the factories and got to experience more of the world. William Henry's problem was he just could not settle and when the regiment came back to England in 1901 he discharged himself. He went back to his job as a carpenter, but struggled to re-adjust in civvy street. In December 1902 he re-enlisted with the South Staffordshire Regiment and served another fifteen months in South Africa. When the regiment returned to home soil in 1905, he was homesick again and transferred to the reserve and came back to Walsall. [176] [177]

My sister, Sarah Bullers died in the summer of 1900, she was just sixty-one years old. This made me the oldest person of the old Reeves family still alive. This elder statesman role of the family, was a position I didn't apply for and didn't particularly want. It just served to remind me of how mortal we really are and how old I was becoming. Sarah only ever had the one child, William and she had been on her own as a widow for a number of years. [178]

The whole nation fell into mourning after the death of our very own Queen Victoria on the 22nd January 1901. She had been queen since 1837 and was the only monarch I had ever known. Her face had been on every coin for sixty-three years. It was the end of an era, but I suppose thats what era's do, end! Bertie, Prince of Wales succeeded as Edward VII and was crowned at Westminster Abbey on the 9th August 1902.

To snapshot the family in spring 1901. My own family lived in West Bromwich Street, Walsall. I was working as a bricklayers labourer to support my four youngest children; Enoch, twelve; Arthur, eleven; David, nine and Annie, six. My daughter Rose Lilian, who was seventeen had just married her husband Orlando Smith and they were both living with me. [179] Also at my family hotel was my half-brother Edward Hammond who was estranged from his wife. He had formed a relationship with my daughter Frances and they were expecting their first child. The church did not class their relationship as incest, but the law prevented their close relationship marriage. I wasn't entirely happy about the situation, but Edward was always vulnerable. It was the lesser of two evils, having him here with me, or letting him get mixed up with his own brother Jim. Edward was nineteen years older than Frances, but she was the one with all the sense. Their first two children, both named Edward Hammond Reeves died shortly after birth in 1901 and 1902. [180] [181][182] [183] They thought they had been cursed and I'm certain my mother would have had a view on the situation. My youngest brother Abel lived in the Meeting Yard off Dudley Street with his wife Sophia and their children Abel, William, Enoch, Lillian and May. [184] Abel's eldest two children by his first marriage had moved away. His son, Thomas was working on the railways in Birmingham and was married to Florence Wootton. [185] [186] Abel's daughter Sarah Jane Reeves was married to Florence's brother, Alfred Wootton and also lived in Birmingham. [187] [188] Jim Hammond was living in Bank Street with his wife Lucy and children Thomas, Enoch and Nellie. [189] The Jones family still lived a few doors away from them.

Abel and Sophia's eldest son, John Thomas Reeves was working on a farm in Cheshire, he never saw eye to eye with his father. [190] He

111

joined the South Staffordshire Territorial's, before enlisting with the regular Royal Regiment of Artillery to get away from Walsall. Not long after, he deserted and moved to Cheshire on the farm to keep out of the way. Despite being a deserter, he went back to the army using the surname Reeve in 1903, enlisting with the Army Service Corp as a driver. He served another three years in the military by which time, he must have thought it safe to return to his home town of Walsall. In 1907, John Thomas married Ada Alice Thorpe, the sister of Susan who was married to my step-son Robert Stanton. [191] There were nine girls and no boys in the Thorpe family and I always wondered how the father managed with all those women, or maybe he had it very easy. [192] [193] [194]

In February 1905, my son, Enoch enlisted with the South Staffords about the same time as his elder brother William Henry joined the reserve. [195] In October 1905, Arthur followed him into the same regiment, they really were true brothers in arms. I was really proud that they both left Walsall to serve their country. They could only benefit from seeing the world, in a way I did in my own youth. I was assured that they would at sometime return much stronger, better men.

The next instalment of the Hammond's saga was never that far away. Just before six o'clock on the morning of Thursday the 17th November 1904, Jim and his next door neighbour Frederick Bond were caught by Sergeant Nunn on private land at Calderfields. The sergeant with a couple of his men grabbed hold of them both, while trying to hide under a wall. They were caught red handed with eight freshly killed rabbits, together with the nets and pegs. At court Jim had no choice but to plead guilty, Bond said it was "a bad job they were there". Both received fines of ten shillings with costs and their nets were confiscated. [196]

On the 17th June 1906, Jim's two sons, Enoch who was seventeen and Edward who was sixteen were caught with two other boys playing cards in the street for money. This was done blatantly and blasphemously on a Sunday as people went to church. They were all summoned to court on Wednesday the 27th June. Police constable Donlan told the bench that he had received numerous complaints about street gambling in the area. When he first saw the boys they immediately ran off. Then about twenty minutes later, he caught the younger boy John Kennedy who had the cards and five and a half pennies in his teeth. Enoch Hammond said he was there standing nearby but was not playing because he had no money. Edward said he was not with his brother at the time. A witness Mrs. Jones told the court that Edward was in her house at the time. The chief constable smelt a rat and recognised Mrs. Jones as one of the Hammond clan. She was Matilda Jones, Edward Hammond's aunt. He asked her outright, "Hasn't your husband been convicted for poaching, Isn't he an associate of poachers?" She replied "No sir". The chief constable was not convinced and told her, "You know Hammond, hasn't he a weakness for poaching. Is it a case of birds of a feather, that is all." He strongly implied to the court that the evidence was false and from a family member, a bird of the feather. The chief constable stated that the elder Hammond had been convicted of gaming before. Edward Hammond was acquitted, the Bench accepting that there was a doubt in his case. The others were fined one shilling and costs. [197]

By 1907 poaching was rife across the whole of Walsall and the south Staffordshire region with Jim Hammond sitting at the top of the criminal tree. At the age of fifty-one he was the most notorious villain in Walsall, a seasoned career criminal with a time served reputation. The police desperately wanted to pluck the Hammond thorn from their side because the gang continued to get away with moonlight robbery. The poachers, unmercifully ravaged the local gentry's lands, nothing was safe from their thieving hands. To the constabulary, Jim was their antagonising wasp, bringing complaints to their door. Though he lived in Walsall, he committed crime deep into the Staffordshire farmlands and countryside. Hammond always seemed to be two steps in front of the authorities and with look outs all over the place, they were egged on to commit more daring raids. The police knew Hammond ran the show, but rarely had a chance to catch him in the act. He was never going to stop, in fact he made a good living out of his trade. Though he was occasionally sent to gaol, he saw it as only a minor inconvenience, just an occupational hazard he tried to avoid. He was always on his guard, suspicious and cautious about being 'grassed up' by some suspected informer to Walsall Police. He believed it was the only way the police could keep turning up to catch him red handed. Just as the police wanted him, he wanted the 'little bird' who whispered in their ear. Jim's problem was he poached on land belonging to rich and influential men, who had friends in high places. These people made waves for the chief constable, pressuring him to get results. To the wealthy, Jim Hammond and his mob of men were no better than venomous vermin scurrying across their land in the dead of night like rats. One of the men suffering from the effects of the Hammond's crimes was Sir William Pearman Smith, a Walsall solicitor who owned the Park Hall estate. As a previous Mayor of Walsall from 1899–1902, he had some very influential contacts. Poachers were plaguing his estate and he made numerous complaints to the police about them stripping his land of game. Using his position he called in favours from his friends to sort out his problem. Before long, the chief constable of Walsall, Alexander Thomson was in the firing line from the society bigwigs. His Staffordshire Constabulary counterpart was Superintendent Barrett who was also having constant ear bashings about poachers running riot in his area. The two men met at Rushall to discuss Hammond, who was their mutual target, They started to formulate a plan to rid themselves of his presence. Barrett had a great deal of local knowledge and had first come into contact with the Hammond's way back in 1884. He wanted to take the lead of the joint police operation, which was agreed by Walsall's Chief Constable. Walsall Borough Police detectives were

114

tasked to help bring Jim Hammond back down to earth. They were to question any Hammond associate who happened to find themselves in the cells and in need of a friend. Inducements in return for information were offered and word soon got round, that Jim Hammond had his card marked. Despite this, people feared the Hammond's, even money could not persuade the majority to grass them up. If you lived amongst the Hammond's, then it was far easier to take your punishment from the law, than to take it from them. The police operation began to gather momentum, they only had to be lucky some of the time, while Hammond had to be lucky all of the time. Due to the complaints extra patrols were put in place and gamekeepers were on constant alert. It was only a matter of time before the police were to get lucky.

At about five-thirty in the morning on the 7th August 1907, the Hammond Gang were seen leaving the estate of Sir William Pearman Smith near Green Lane, Sutton Road (There used to be another Green Lane in Walsall now its called Sutton Road, but it ran from the bottom of Princes Avenue to the Broadway). Suspected of trespassing for the purpose of poaching, Police Constable Wright watched as Jim Hammond and three others made off. The officer managed to grab and arrest Hammond, who had six rabbits and a net. The officer recognised another man named Harry Spink and later went to his address in Bott Lane. There he found poaching nets and freshly gathered mushrooms. Samuel Proud from Birmingham Street and James Hammond junior were also prosecuted for being involved. The band appeared together in court on the 16th August 1907, jointly charged with night poaching. Police Constable Wright would not swear that James Hammond junior was one of the men involved, so the case against him was dismissed. The remaining three were described to the bench as well known poachers. Each man was fined forty shillings with costs, or in default one months imprisonment and an order was made for the nets to be destroyed. Fines never got paid, so this bought the police a month of breathing space to pacify the local gentry. [198]

Jim knew that dark forces were working against him so looked and listened for clues as to who the grass might be. What Jim did not know at that point was Walsall Police and Staffordshire Constabulary were jointly working together to bring him down. Behind the scenes Superintendent Barrett was waiting for his next move and upon their release from gaol spies watched to see who greeted them from the gates. Barrett was Jim Hammond's nemesis, their paths had crossed on numerous occasions making them life long adversaries. The superintendent had a near perfect reputation backed up by forty-four years of service in the force. The gang emerged from prison confinement with their security tightened and their guard raised against any further evil betrayals. Any future social meetings were to be at the office, better known as the Walsall Arms in Bank Street, a closed shop to outsiders. Jim cleverly, set little traps by telling all his associates different things. By cunningly remembering who he had told what, he hoped to identify the culprit if anything got back. He would tell 'A' they were going to do a job at 'X' location. He would see if word of it got back and watch for police activity. The job was obviously a ruse and was never going to happen, but 'A' would not know until the last minute cancellation. While determined to evade the police spotlight, he still relished every chance to humiliate the police.

He conceived and hatched a plan to go out even further afield, to even richer pickings of the Staffordshire countryside. Late in September 1907, Jim made a couple of recce runs to fields around the Stonnall area, near Lichfield. He recognised the potential and picked up several ducks and fowl before he returned. What he did not realise was, Superintendent Barrett was a local resident and reports of the thefts soon landed on his desk. At the end of September 1907 the gang met to plan their most audacious raid. They made a pact, sworn between only the trusted few, to keep it as tight as a drum with no leaks. Nobody was to be let in on the job, it was to be strictly on a need to know basis. Jim would only reveal his final plan on the designated night of the raid.

Chapter Nine

The Lynn Affray

J im's much anticipated daring raid was going to be on the night of Friday the 4th October 1907. On that evening they all met up at the Walsall Arms as planned, with the nets in bags ready for the job. With staffs in their hands and armed with stones they were ready to do battle. Each of them swore to fight their way out at any cost if they were cornered. Jim briefed his loyal band of men at the pub, so that everyone knew their parts to play. He watched for the slightest sign of betrayal in their eyes as he set out his plan. With him were his two sons, Ted and Jim junior and his nephew, Abel Reeves. The rest consisted of his old friend Frederick Bond, together with his trusted associates, Samual Proud, Samual Street and John Riley. He had worked with them all before, they were skilled at their craft, but most of all every one was trusted one hundred percent. In any case all of these men had as much to lose if caught as he did. As they raised their glasses to the challenge ahead, Jim told them there was a good walk of about seven and a half miles. Jim knew the countryside and the farmland around Walsall like the back of his hand and kept to the quiet routes to avoid anyones prying eyes. He knew the danger points and he knew the friendly places if they needed to escape. They left the safety of the Walsall Arms and headed off into a starlit night towards Aldridge, taking care of any one paying special interest on their way out. Their spirits were good as they headed towards their intended destination, land in Wood Lane, Stonnall about two hours away. Jim had no suspicions of any betrayal and was confident he was working covertly away from the eyes of the law. The truth was, Walsall Police were aware about the bones of his plan. An informant, perhaps a family member even had stabbed him in the back. As they made their way towards their destination, a reception committee of police and gamekeepers were busy setting their own traps. Word had been sent through to Superintendent Barrett at Staffordshire Police, that a raiding party was on its way. There was only one major objective for the keepers, to capture at all costs the ringleader Jim Hammond. He was a marked man with a price on his head and a target on his back.

The land at Stonnall was owned by John Myatt, but the shooting rights were held by Sir Richard Powell Cooper (1847-1913) Baronet, who resided at the nearby Shenstone Court. Sir Richard trained as a vet and had a surgery in Tamworth Street, Lichfield. He inherited the family business from his uncle and began a large expansion of his estates making land investments around the world, including mines in New Zealand and Africa. In 1889, as a result of his success, he purchased Shenstone Court and was created a baronet in 1905 for services to agriculture. He also owned another family estate at Ashlyns Hall down in Berkhamstead. He was one of the very rich and influential men who complained regularly about the game being stolen for his shooting parties. Sir Richard's head game keeper was the experienced Robert Smith Edwards, who had rounded up his men, George Blake, Henry Pate, Frederick Daniels, and John Haimes. Police Constable Lee from Staffordshire Police was tasked with being in the vicinity, but was only to come to their assistance if things got out of hand. They did not want Hammond to become suspicious about there being a police informer, so the official story would be he was just patrolling the area. By nine-thirty that evening, the briefed and prepared gamekeepers secreted themselves in the area and lay in wait. It was going to be a long night and a long wait. The Hammond gang had spent longer in the Walsall Arms than expected. The keepers patience was to be rewarded at about one o'clock that Saturday morning, when they first had sight of the gang of eight enter the area.

Jim Hammond led his band of poachers into the chosen field sticking close to the hedge line, but had unwittingly taken them into an ambush. The gamekeepers sat tight, watching as the poachers began the process of setting out their nets. Slowly the keepers crept closer and closer towards them, waiting for Robert Smith Edwards to give the signal to rush the Hammond's. As they got to within catching distance the head keeper sprung the trap, calling out, "You better come quietly, as I have plenty of men here." Jim Hammond was not going anywhere peacefully and shouted out to his men, "Come on, the law are here". The gang brought their staffs and stones to hand, intending to fight their way out. All hell broke out, with the keepers making a B-line to grab Jim Hammond. The Hammond gang meanwhile formed a ring of steel to fend them off. George Blake seized his chance to grab Jim Hammond, but was viciously beaten to the ground by Jim junior and his brother Ted. Riley and Street also got stuck in, resulting in Blake being totally overpowered and knocked to the ground. Fearing for his life, Blake screamed, "Come and help me, I'm down." Robert Smith Edwards, panicked when he realised just how tough the Hammond's were and blew his whistle. This signalled Police Constable Lee to come to their immediate assistance. He entered the affray and instantly realised the gravity of the situation. He believed Blake was in serious danger and shouted, "Stop that, you'll kill him". As he approached he was cracked with a stick by one of the gang almost knocking him down. Drawing his truncheon he managed to wrestle Ted Hammond to the ground, where he was arrested and handcuffed. During the struggle the constable was struck with stones and sticks several times about the head and body. He and the keepers desperately fought a battle with the Hammond's for fifteen minutes or so, until the tide slowly turned. The gang then began to scatter, but not before Jim Hammond and Fred Bond were taken prisoner. This was a proper affray and afterwards three-hundred yards of rabbit netting and a quantity of sticks and stones were seized. The rest of the leaderless gang disappeared into the night, furious in the knowledge that they had been trapped and set up again! That violent night produced plenty of bruises and spilt blood on both sides. George Blake was left semi-conscious and senseless on the ground, needing to be stretchered from the field. On the way to Lichfield Police Station, Jim Hammond furiously stared at the bruised and bloody faces of his captures and jeered, "They haven't had it all their own way as it is!" Hammond gave his son, Ted and Fred Bond the signal to say nothing to the police. He must have thought they had killed Blake such was the beating he received. Bond showed no remorse when he told Police Constable Lee, "I wish I'd got my battle axe with me; I'd finish some of you". The rest of the bedraggled gang made the slow walk back to Walsall, the worse for their beating and knowing that the law would be fast on their heels.

The three were banged up in the cells all night, until the following morning, Saturday the 5th October 1907. After Jim had been woken he reminded the others to stay quiet in case the police were listening. After drinking some cold water they were dragged up the steps to the court. The Lichfield Magistrates sitting at the County Police Court were told the bare bones of the circumstances in the briefest hearing. The police told magistrates that a number of outstanding offenders were still at large. The bench had no hesitation in remanding the defendants into custody for a week, allowing the police to make further enquiries and arrests. Unlike hearings at Walsall, there were no friendly faces in the public gallery to make whitty quips. The three were dragged unceremoniously back down to the cells.

Back in Walsall the rest of the gang kept their heads down, waiting to see what happened next. They had all agreed to keep quiet and deny everything if caught. They remained quietly confident that the gamekeepers and police could not possibly know their identities. They knew their comrades would not ever give them up, but at the same time

121

sensed something was terribly amiss. They would not have long to find out. The police not only had their names, they knew where to find them. In fact the police had already been to court to obtain warrants in all their names. The police apparently knew everything. The explanation was staring them in the face, beyond all doubt, someone had been an informer.

On the morning of Monday the 7th October 1907, Police Constable Lee and Sergeant Needham went to Radley Cottages, Rushall, the home address of Samuel Street and John Riley. Samual Proud was also there when the door was knocked. Riley opened the door and declaring his innocence said, "Why do you always come here, I might as well do something". He was instantly identified by Police Constable Lee as one of the offenders. This unnerved them, how could he say for sure. That night when Blake was assaulted, it was pitch black. Both Street and Riley were arrested, but claimed they didn't know Proud. The officers asked Proud a few questions, but while they were busy detaining Riley and Street, he seized the chance to escape.

At Rushall police station the two men were strip searched. Sergeant Needham noted that Street had distinctive weal marks across his back, consistent with being in a recent fight. At the time of being charged, Street said, "You've made a mistake this time."

At about eight o'clock on the evening of Tuesday the 8th October 1907, Police Constable Lee went to Walsall town centre looking for other members of the gang. He was accompanied by Detective Constable Lloyd from Walsall Borough Police, Sergeant Parsons from Brownhills Police and Robert Smith Edwards. Police Constable Lee recognised Abel Reeves as one of the gang, walking along the street. After being arrested he said, "I have never been poaching in my life, I don't know what poaching is." He was wearing a coat with a truncheon pocket and two large poachers pockets, containing traces of rabbit fur. He claimed he bought the coat recently for sixpence, but couldn't remember the seller's identity. He was escorted to his home address where a search of his premises was conducted. They recovered a large bag covered in fur containing a number of rabbit skins. On a roll, they went to Jim Hammond's home address around the corner. They found three men there, one being Jim Hammond junior who Police Constable Lee identified as another one of the violent poachers. When arrested he dismissed the seriousness by saying, "Well, that ain't much, they can't blumin hang me for that." His mother reassured him by saying, "Keep your pecker up, Jim. I'll get some witnesses like I did before." Another man said as they left, "Keep your mouth shut, and they can't do much then." The cousins, Jim Hammond and Abel Reeves were taken to Brownhills police station, where they were held over night in the cells. Whilst sitting in their cold cells, they must have wondered how the police knew their every movement. On Wednesday the 9th October 1907, James Hammond junior, Abel Reeves, Samuel Street and John Riley appeared before the Brownhills Petty Sessions charged with night poaching with violence. They looked at each other in astonishment when they saw Superintendent Barrett in court who asked the bench to remand them all in custody. They knew Superintendent Barrett had taken an active interest in the Hammond's for a considerable time. Jim junior knew Barrett had been after his dad for years. He knew he had history dating back to July 1884, when his dad and uncle Ben got locked up at Streetly, some twenty-three years earlier. Barrett's presence reaffirmed a realisation that some bitter collusion had taken place with the police, but the mystery was who?

All seven defendants came up before Lichfield Police Court on the morning of Saturday the 12th October 1907, where some of the evidence was heard. George Blake was still too ill to appear in person and Superintendent Barrett said an eighth man Samuel Proud, was implicated but had not yet been arrested. The seven men were remanded in custody for another week. From the dock, Jim Hammond stared straight at his old adversary, Superintendent Barrett and knew he had been had. The look between the two was very deep, Barrett with the smugness of victory and Jim a glare of revenge. There was little doubt the superintendent had orchestrated this investigation and was now controlling things. Walsall Magistrates were well versed in the antics and stunts pulled by the Hammonds and soon their colleagues at Lichfield were about to find out.

Lichfield magistrates sat at a special County Police Court on Saturday the 19th October 1907, to continue hearing the evidence against all of the men. Mr. Arthur Chetwynd was chairman of the bench and he was accompanied by Colonel H. D. Williams. Jim Hammond secured the attendance of his solicitor Mr. G. Bailey from the firm, Stanley and Jackson of Walsall and Mr. G. Ashmall appeared to prosecute the case on behalf of the police. Before the case began Mr. Bailey stated that his clients had no case to answer in respect of the violence. This was because the gamekeepers had no power of arrest as their employer did not own the land. In fact he claimed they had all been unlawfully arrested. Reluctantly, Mr. Ashmole was forced to concede that in law he was right. The loophole in the law had been exploited again and they agreed the charge must be reduced to a lesser offence of unlawful trespass for the purpose of taking and destroying game at night. The defendants were then brought into the courtroom and the clerk read out the lesser charge and asked for their plea. They had big smiles on their faces, but Superintendent Barrett was less than amused by the turn of events. He just sat quietly at the back of the court, monitoring proceedings whilst making his presence obvious to the defendants. To the lesser charge, Frederick Bond, James Hammond, and Ted Hammond who were all caught in the act pleaded guilty, but the rest entered a not guilty plea.

Mr. Ashmall prosecuting, opened his case by telling the magistrates the charge was reduced after some consideration and hesitation, but mainly so they could decide the outcome that day. The purpose was to save the expense and trouble of sending the prisoners for trial at the higher court of Quarter Sessions. He said a large amount of violence was used against Blake which could easily have proven a lot more serious. Mr. Ashmall strongly advocated that a severe punishment was necessary, if only to act as a deterrent to night poachers who had become the scourge of Shenstone. Mr. Bailey protested furiously that Mr. Ashmall's comments were misleading. He made it clear that the charge had been reduced purely as a matter of law and nothing else. He adamantly reminded the court that in law, the gamekeepers had no power to arrest his clients at all. He also strongly objected to the prosecution mentioning the matter of violence, especially as this element had been dropped from the case. The bench seemed somewhat unhappy that Mr. Bailey had won this point. Either way he didn't want to annoy them further, so continued to conduct the defence based on the alibis he had been given. The witnesses were presented one-by-one to the court giving evidence in chief.

The first up for the prosecution was Dr. Manfield from Shenstone, who said he had examined George Blake, on the Tuesday 8th October 1907 at his home in Footherley. He recounted that Blake was in bed with a wound to the right eye lid, very close to the eye. He also had bruises on both arms and legs and great tenderness and pain in the region of the spleen and kidney. The doctor considered the injuries and internal pains to be severe and a direct result of the violent kicking and punching he received. Blake had to remain in bed until Sunday the 13th October 1907 but was still not able to return to work.

Mr. Bailey put Robert Smith Edwards, head keeper under the spotlight when he asked why Police Constable Lee was in the vicinity at the time. He wondered why at this rural location some distance away from either town or village the police were patrolling in the dead of night. It was clear he suspected his clients had been set up by the police, possibly with the help of an informant. When asked Smith Edwards said they were expecting poachers. Before he could ask why he expected them, the Chairman intervened by saying, "if you lived in Shenstone you were bound to expect poachers all the time" and laughed. This effectively stopped this line of questioning. It was clear the Bench had taken a dislike to Mr. Bailey's tone and his big town defence tactics. Despite believing the magistrates disliked him, he went on to suggest there was something irregular or underhanded about the way things were done by the police. He asked, how it was possible for his clients names to have appeared on the warrants even before they had been formerly identified. This was despite their identities being unknown to the gamekeepers or police. He said they only went to Riley's cottage because they knew it was a place the police usually went to find poachers. Mr. Bailey made it clear he suspected a 'Stitch Up', but said the apparent positive identifications had put him in an awkward position leaving him no alternative than to proceed on the basis this was a case of mistaken identity.

The defence then began to bring their own witnesses. Samuel Street told the court that on the night in question he was at home and went to bed at about eleven o'clock. He got up at about five-fifty the following morning and went to work. He told the court that he knew nothing at all about poaching and had never done any in his life. He venomously denied he was at Lynn on the night in question. Alice Street, his wife confirmed that her husband never went out of the house all night. Mr. Ashmall cross-examining asked him about the weal marks on his back, to which he said they were caused by a fall of rocks at work about six months previously. John Riley was next up in the box, who claimed he was at home digging up potatoes from his garden until he went to bed at about ten-thirty in the evening. He was there all night until about five-fifty, when he decided to make a short day at the colliery on the Saturday morning as he had not been to work all week. The Chairman said he found it very strange, Riley should dig up potatoes on work days and go to work on half days. Emma Riley, his wife enforced that she and her husband went to bed together at about ten o'clock on the night in question and he was still in bed when she woke about five o'clock in the morning. At various times the magistrates looked at each other in disbelief, they seemed to dislike all the Walsall residents who they suspected were accomplished liars. James Hammond, junior, said he went to bed that night sometime between eleven and eleven-thirty. He did not get up until quarter to eight the following morning for work at Wednesbury. Amelia Hammond, his wife said, she woke up twice during the night and her husband was in bed each time. His landlady Eliza Record told the magistrates that she gave him a call for work at quarter to eight. She would have heard him get up, because there was a creaky door on his room and she slept on the same floor. Eliza Record was his sister, but this was not mentioned to the court. The atmosphere was one of a stage show and the magistrates were tiring of the performances. In the interests of fairness the trial continued but the outcome was being determined with every word spoken.

Abel Reeves claimed he went to bed at about eleven-thirty that evening and did not leave his bedroom until seven-thirty the following morning. Having initially gone to work, he left early and went for a walk around the town with a friend. He said, the alleged 'poachers coat' was purchased for his tackle when he went fishing. His wife, Mary Reeves told the court on oath, that Abel was in bed each time she woke at quarter to one, twenty past three and at five to six. She said there were no rabbit skins in the house when the police arrived, so they must have been planted by them. After giving her evidence, the chairman commented that it was very clear she told lies from beginning to end. He said her testimony was unbelievable and not a word of it was barely worth wasting time listening to. Samuel Proud told the court a ridiculous story that he was a single man, who went to the Temperance

Hall before having two half pints of ale on the way home. The show continued for five long hours until the Bench retired to consider their verdict. Their minds must have been made up long before the end. After only a short absence for deliberations the magistrates returned to the courtroom with stern faces. Glaring at the men at the back in the dock, Mr. Chetwynd told them they were very lucky that violence had been dropped from the charge. He reminded them that such a serious case could have been heard at the Court of Assizes, where they would have been imprisoned for fourteen years. He said he personally lived in the area and had first hand knowledge of the damage done by theft and the evils of poaching. Showing little signs of sympathy with the defendants, he told them their criminal records strongly suggested involvement in numerous similar crimes. He also believed they were most likely to be the gentlemen who emptied all the hen roosts in the area. Frederick Bond, James Hammond and Ted Hammond received sentences of three months imprisonment, Samuel Proud two months and the rest one month each. All sentences of imprisonment were given with the conditions of additional hard labour! Mr. Bailey made an application that the nets should be returned. The Chairman said, "if you can get them, you can have them, but we make no order" and laughed.

The fact was, Arthur Chetwynd's privileged world as chairman of the bench was a million miles away from the backstreets of Walsall. He was the grandson of George Chetwynd, 2nd Baronet Chetwynd of Brocton Hall. He himself resided at Longdon Hall and was the land agent for 6th Marquess of Anglesey, who owned the nearby Beaudesert Hall. His sister, Florence had married Berkeley Charles Sydney Paget (born 1844), youngest son of Henry Paget, 2nd Marquess of Anglesey. He was most likely talking about himself as a 'victim' of the poachers when he delivered his verdict.

Superintendent George Barrett retired from Staffordshire Constabulary at the age of seventy in March 1909, having served for forty-six years. [199] He died on Christmas Eve 1923 aged eighty-five at his home at Muckley Corner and was buried at Stonnall on the 29th December. [200] [201] [202] [203] [204] [205] [206] [207] [208] [209] [210]

Chapter Ten

Westward Bound

The Hammond's had been stung by a covert police operation, obviously pre-empted by a tip off, everybody knew it, including me. Despite his best efforts, Jim had been betrayed again and he knew it was someone close to him. I thought my connections with old colleagues, would frame me in Jim's spotlight of suspicion. He must have realised by raising the stakes with threats of violence, he would attract the laws attention. His activities had become a nuisance to the chief constable, who had become annoyed with all the complaints he was getting. In response to the grievances the chief had authorised his detectives to start paying for credible information. Although he knew it was someone close, who could it have been, it still wasn't easy to figure it out. There were several motives why people wanted Jim stopped, justice, revenge, spite or simple criminal competition. Whatever it was, someone cared little if Jim and his men got sent down. To be honest, for a long time he had been asking for it, he had become cocky and thought he was invincible. He couldn't blame anybody but himself, but he was puzzled and confused how anybody found out about the job, when he had been so careful. He knew I didn't know anything, unless someone had told me, but was happy nobody would ever do that. He was always careful to remind people of my past police service and never to talk business in front of me. Jim did however confide in his brother Edward, who was living with my daughter Frances. Although Edward didn't get involved in Jim's business, he was still his brother and did receive some of the ill gotten gains from him. Edward would never betray Jim knowingly, Jim trusted him despite his association to me. Edward was also careful never to say anything about Jim's business to me. Not that he did not trust me, he just never wanted me to be put in a difficult position, especially before my retirement from the police. Frances was always worried that Jim's influence would take Edward off the rails. She tried her best to keep him in check and away from his brothers gang. Frances came to me when she was worried about the gangs raids, she thought that sooner or later Edward would be tarred with the same brush. Jim never believed in a million years that Edward would tell Frances anything to get him locked up, but he did. You are probably wondering now if I dobbed them in, well the police never disclose the identity of the informant, it's a well known fact. The truth is, I do know the answer but some things are better taken to the grave, nobody needs to know for sure.

After this law breaking escapade, I'd had more than enough of the Hammond's and had come to my own decision to get away from the mess. I was going to leave Walsall for a second time, just like I did in 1859. This time I was going to leave Walsall and England for yet another new continent. I suppose most people think the grass is greener at times in their lives, but I was at a crossroads of life and realised it was now or never. At my age, I knew time was not on my side, I was over the brow of the hill and half way down the other side. I didn't have any major ties apart from the two kids, everyone else was either grown up or dead including my poor Sarah. No one had been told yet and I was apprehensive about what the kids were going to say. I really thought it was time for me to turn the page and move on. I wasn't going to let it look as though I was running away though, Jim could never prove anything, he was never going to get the satisfaction of thinking it was me for sure. My brother Enoch had successfully made a new life for himself in Salt Lake City and the prospect of a change of scenery appealed to me. Enoch told me that there was plenty of work out in America and it would be a great place to bring the children up in the land of freedom and opportunity. I thought about it long and hard, but my mind was all but made up.

Jim came out of prison in January 1908 and at the age of fifty-two, life was beginning to show on his face. Prison hard labour for three months had added to his woes and he was no longer a spring chicken. He came to me surprisingly almost cap in hand and asked me if I could help him find out who grassed him up. He was quite humble and sincere and it was a genuine cry for help. He didn't think it was me after all, I was quite taken back and surprised he didn't accuse me outright. He was always a confrontational kind of man and rarely thought too much about things before he acted. He was desperate to get his hands on the turncoat who cost him his liberty and hoped I would be able to find out from my police sources. I told him that there was no way they would tell me, police information was vital and they were very protective. He said he was certain it was something to do with Barrett, the superintendent from Brownhills and he vowed to find the 'grass'. I told him that Staffordshire Police was a completely different force to Walsall, but he begged me to keep my ears open anyway. At the end of the day, he fought the law and the law won. It was the natural mechanism to maintain the status quo in the world. I was sorry that he had suffered in prison, but I had very little sympathy. He was after all the author of his own misfortune.

With the money I had put aside, I booked three second-class tickets with the prestigious White Star line, for me, my son David and daughter Annie. I sent and received several letters from Enoch and there was no going back, this was going to be my chance to escape. We were going to sail on the SS Republic from Liverpool on the 14th November 1908, bound for Boston and then on to meet my brother in Salt Lake City, Utah. [211] I had not seen Enoch for eighteen years and hoped I would find him well and not too much changed since I saw him last.

I told my eldest son, William Henry about the tickets I had bought to see his uncle Enoch in America. William worked as a carpenter and was still single, but got married the following year. I asked him to look after the rest of the family. It was time for me to hand over the family reins which I had held onto, for far too long. He asked me, "Are you ever coming back, dad," and looked me right in the eye. I just said, "I don't know son, but the truth is, probably not!". He had a sad look on his face, but he also understood and respected my decision. I wrote to the boys, Enoch and Arthur who were still serving with the South Staffords to explain things. I knew they had their own lives and didn't need me for support anymore. My stepson Robert was thirty-eight and lived with his wife and four children. He was visibly upset at my leaving, I had always been the father he never had but we agreed to write and stay in regular touch. My daughter Frances now had four sons with my half-brother Edward. Edward though older than Frances relied on her, she was stronger than him in every way. I think all the business with Jim had persuaded Edward to stay on the right side of the law, once and for all. Frances was deeply saddened by my decision and knew I was never coming back by the look on my face. It felt as if I was abandoning her and that thought pained my conscience. I had always been her confidant and would miss our chats about the world. To be fair this was the heaviest wrench for my heart strings. Rose had three little ones and shed a tear when I told her my news. She was a lot like her mother Sarah and wished me good luck. I knew deep down she would never say anything to hold me back, she was that kind of girl. I told my two youngest children, David who was sixteen and Annie who was fourteen. Both sorely missed growing up with their mother absent and had mixed feelings. Annie was at an age that she really needed Sarah's presence and was less than happy about leaving. David was quite pleased about the adventure as he did not see much of a future for himself in Walsall. I realised it was a big wrench taking them away

133

from everything they had known, away from the memories of their mother could not have been easy for either of them.

The youngest of my brothers, Abel wished me well as did his son, Enoch who was seventeen and shook my hand saying, "keep smiling uncle H, one day you might come back". Perhaps the young lad knew something I didn't. Edward told Jim that I was going before I got the chance to say anything to him first. He came round and said, "I hear you're going," I told him I was going to see Enoch in the United States. He asked, "You ever coming back H, there's not much here for you, so I suppose its, good luck." The old rogue, awkward as our relationship had been over the years, left by saying, "keep out the oss rowd". For the first time in a long time, I felt that despite all our differences, we were still brothers. Maybe it was a feeling sent to me by mum, but our parting was at least on good terms. I did one last round of all my old friends and acquaintances at the beginning of November 1908 and that was that. Just one thing remained to be done, a visit to mums grave to say goodbye to her. As I walked out of the cemetery there was a lump in my throat, but I still had my memories in my old kit bag. Memories don't belong to a place, they belong to a person and mine were packed ready to go. I was now ready for the next adventure.

On the morning of the 13th November 1908 our few packed possessions were hauled to the railway station on the coldest of days. A couple of the family and a few old friends shouted their farewells along the way. We waited for the train to arrive to begin our journey to the port of Liverpool. When we took our seats I made a mental note of the station for one last time. The whistle blew, the train chugged and steamy smoke bellowed out for the last time in the old place I called home. My mind was flooded with all the memories as I saw the town slowly disappear. It's fair to say we were all apprehensive, so arriving near the port of Liverpool we stayed overnight in some dingy digs. On the morning of the 14th November 1908, we made our way to line up in the queue at the White Star docking area with our tickets in hand. The SS Republic was a grand ship and looked huge sitting in the dock with its four masts and large central funnel. It was still only five years old and was a palatial class of vessel used by American millionaires. I think the very sight of it was awe inspiring for the kids, who had never seen such a great machine in the flesh. They seemed particularly quiet at the prospect of getting aboard, the sight had literally took the wind out of their sails. The reality had set in, this was now very real, we were going and could smell the ocean. Having checked our tickets we were allowed to climb the gangplank up to the deck, where the staff pointed us towards our second class accommodation. We were billeted in a small cabin for the next eight days on our voyage towards Boston, Massachusetts in the United States of America. Our accommodation was fairly good, based on my experiences of the old army troop carriers, they smelt better as well. Our cabin was perfectly acceptable, I don't know what the third-class bunks were like and I wasn't in a hurry to find out. Although I often thought about travelling, I didn't think it would be when I was a sixty-five year old widower. I thought after marrying Sarah, I was totally settled down, roots and all. Life cruelly reminded me that nothing lasts for ever and roots can be ripped out in the cruel storm of life. I did tell the White Star line that I was sixty-two, hoping it would improve my prospects of work, or perhaps they misheard, it's easily done. On the deck of the ship, I felt the wind of change in my white hair and really hoped the United States would be a clean break and fresh start for us all. We all needed to just getaway and this was doing it in style. This after all was a fantastic experience for David and Annie although I wasn't sure how long the euphoria would last.

The sea crossing went relatively well and we sailed into Boston port on the morning of the 22nd November 1908. It was a cold morning as we left the ship, lugging our belongings along behind us like refugees.

Salt Lake City was over two thousand miles away from Boston, we had only just reached the half way point. A several day journey on the railroad lay ahead of us before we would reach our final destination. The prospect reminded me of the long trek to Beijing years before, that seemed to last an eternity. I just hoped we would be blessed with the feeling of adventure and not endurance. We got aboard the train at Boston and travelled first to Albany then on to Buffalo. It was a long old route and at various times my fellow travellers fell asleep to the lullaby of the train rumbling along the tracks. From Buffalo we went to Cleveland, travelling near to the Great Lake Erie. The parallel rails led us eventually to Chicago on the banks of the Great Lake Michigan. Our train finally came to a halt when we landed at La Salle Street Station. This trip took us just over two days so I decided to stop for a day in some local digs, while I worked out our next leg to Salt Lake City. The United States is a vast landscape and travelling was a tiring experience for us all. There was so much to take in, spectacular scenery where everything seemed to have been created on a much bigger scale. This was the big country, a place our forefathers fought to win all the way to the far western side. My old king and queen coins had been replaced by eagles and strange faces. I purchased the tickets for the final stage of our journey and we walked to the station to catch the train. As the steam train arrived at the platform you could hear the ding, ding, ding, ding of the train bell as it came hissingly to a halt. We climbed aboard and as we pulled away, bid Chicago a fond farewell. We travelled through to Omaha, then Cheyenne, then Ogden before finally arriving at Salt Lake City. This excursion took ages, with us sleeping and eating when we could get chance. Excitement seemed to increase the closer we got to Salt Lake City. Don't get me wrong, some of the places we visited were pretty grim and it was great to leave them behind, but it was all part of the journey.

Salt Lake City was predominantly a Mormon city and only about sixty years old. It was built by the early Mormon religious settlers as their American centre. Many originated from the old country so had similar thinking to us. They had practiced polygamy for years something that only finally stopped in 1904. This made me think about the many bigamous marriages in the old town, but they normally only lived with one spouse at a time. It was however a well established city and capital of the Utah state. The main street was lined with electricity and telegraph poles and the street had tram lines running its length. There were horses and carriages everywhere but the streets were wide and spacious, not like the old town of Walsall. My brother lived on South Sixth West Street with his wife Mary Jane and his son Alfred, who was sixteen. Alfred was the first of the Reeves family born in the United States, having come along late in the marriage when my brother and his wife were both in their early forties. Enoch owned his own brass foundry in the city and had made a good living for himself. His daughter Mary Jane, was thirty-four and had married a few months earlier in September 1908.

It was fantastic to see Enoch's face as we walked out of the railroad stations precinct. At fifty-eight he had noticeably aged since our last meeting, but I suppose the passing of time had changed us all. He was overjoyed and eager to take us to his house, which was surprisingly large and modern. We had a family meal and talked for hours about the old days in Walsall with mother and the rest of the family. He had so many questions about the family and just wanted an all round catch up. We both laughed saying how funny it was that we ended up so far away from Walsall. Alfred and David were both of a similar age and seemed to get on well which was nice to see. I could see the difference in the two upbringings and hoped for good things. I had a good feeling that David was going to settle in well to his new environment. I soon got a permanent roof over our head on North Fifth West Street and got work fairly easily as a watchman on the roadworks. It suited me working shifts including nights, because I had more time with the family during the day. I never needed that much sleep and with the passing of time needed even less. This place really was a million miles away from Walsall.

I'm sure guardian angels must watch over us at certain times in our lives, ancestors from the past protecting their own on the journey of life. In January 1909 the tragic front page news spread all across America of the demise and sinking of the SS Republic. We had all sailed on the vessels last successful voyage. On the 20th January 1909, the SS Republic had set off again from New York destined for the Mediterranean. At about four-thirty in the morning on the 23rd January, as the liner sailed through thick fog fifty miles from Nantucket Island, it was rammed in the port side by the Italian owned liner SS Florida. Two people, Mrs. Lynch and Mr. Langdon both American's, were killed in the impact and several others were injured. The Republic immediately began to take on water and mayday distress signals were sent out using the recently installed Marconi radio system. Jack Binns the operator continually sent out messages despite the severe damage to the radio deck and the threat of the roof falling in on him at any time. Captain Sealby ordered the lifeboats to be made ready. Four hundred and sixty-one passengers were transferred without panic to the less damaged Florida. The Republic's sister ship, SS Baltic arrived and a decision was made to take on the passengers from both ships due to the considerable damage to SS Florida's bow. Twenty lifeboats began conveying the passengers from the Florida. At one point some of the Italian immigrant passengers began to panic and made selfish runs for the boats. A steward named Spencer from the Republic knocked several of them out in the human stampede, until an officer drew his revolver in order to restore order to the proceedings. The wind picked up making it a daunting experience for the passengers and it was still dark. The thick fog and drenching rain made the rescue conditions treacherous. The rolling sea made the Baltic gangplank a challenging task for poor soaking wet souls to get aboard. One young girl fell in the icy water, only to be saved at the last attempt by a sailor with a hook, who heaved her from the depths. The Revenue Cutter Gresham came to attempt a tow back to shore, while most of the crew volunteered to remain on board the Republic with the captain. At seven o'clock as the situation worsened the captain ordered all crew to leave. With the exception of the second officer, Mr. Williams they manned the lifeboats and were picked up by the Gresham. At eight o'clock the bow began to rise and the ship began its final decent. A lifeboat was dispatched from the Gresham to save the captain and second officer. They were found clinging to the wreckage for dear life, neither wearing life vests. Mr. Williams was washed into the sea when a big wave hit him. He was plucked out of the water at the last attempt, just before he gave up hope. The captain clung on until the last seconds, just before the ship went down and was rescued just in time. Unfortunately the coffins containing the two dead were still on the deck when the ship went down. This was the first time in maritime history that Marconi radio had been used to save life at sea. It was hailed a great advancement in safety at sea. [212] [213]

Oddly on the trip before ours a young girl named Annie Rooney from Ireland committed suicide by inexplicably slitting her own throat with a razor. Maybe this was an omen of bad things to come. After the ship went down to its deep dark grave, stories started about a mysterious legend. It was said that it sank with gold bullion worth millions in the vaults! I'm just glad we did not have to experience that ordeal. I took a moment to thank my guardian angels for our safe trip.

There was a great start to the year in 1909 with us settling well into our new surroundings. Like the rest of my story, there were lots of peaks and troughs and the next down turn was never far away. Perhaps

I missed the signs, but I failed to realise that my daughter Annie, now fourteen was becoming a woman. She really needed Sarah her mother, instead she had an aged old soldier for a father and surrogate mother. I didn't grasp her age and her coming maturity, I only saw her awkwardness and disobedience. At the time I didn't comprehend that I was failing her miserably. I thought working every hour to provide for David and Annie, took care of all their needs. I was wrong and things came to a head on the evening of the 23rd July 1909. I had a blazing row with Annie, she was like a woman possessed and flew at me saying she never wanted to leave Walsall and blamed me for everything that was wrong in her life. She ran from the house barefoot in a fit of temper and hysteria. I went out with David looking for her, but couldn't find her anywhere. I honestly feared the worst until she returned. We didn't speak as I thought, "least said, soonest mended," but before the morning came she was gone again.

I contacted the police to report her missing only to be informed she had been picked up on Sixth West Street, near First South Street by a Mr. Burrell in a terrible state. He had taken her to the emergency hospital believing she had taken some kind of poison bringing on her incoherent madness. Annie told police officers I was responsible for battering and choking her before she ran away. It's true I had been firm and tried to stop her leaving in a state, but I loved her and had read the situation wrong. She told Mr. Burrell she was going to drown herself in the Jordon River which runs through the city. I suppose he saved her life and thank God he did. I could never have forgiven myself had anything bad happened. Dr. Stewart at the hospital managed to calm her down and after speaking to her got to the truth of what really happened. That morning the facts of the case were heard in the Juvenile Court who had to make a decision about her safety. The court concluded I was right to reprimand her behaviour and returned her back to my custody. They sympathised with the family make-up and the lack of a mothers guiding hand. It was a sad time, but I was determined to try my best to help her through these challenging times. [214] [215]

Annie always considered herself older than she actually was, but to be fair she needed to be. I could do little to control her hormonal outbursts at me and wished Sarah was with me to help me through. It is never easy to be a father and mother to a teenager. Thinking back, I had overlooked the fact that in 1899 her mother had died and coming to America elevated her to the woman of the house. It was all too much and I blame myself for not seeing her distress.

The following year Annie got married to John Eaves, who was ten years older than her. [216] [217] She was only fifteen at the time she married, which was legal in Utah. By the February of 1911 she had her first child, Mary Annie. It's never easy when the day arrives in a man's life that you realise your usefulness to others is at an end. I had to accept that my children were grown and now had control of their own destiny.

In May 1910 word came that the king Edward VII was dead, he had spent so long in his mothers shadow that he was king for but nine years. He was succeeded by his son George V.

Back in the old country, life went on in that smoky town of Walsall and some things never changed. The Hammond's poaching exploits carried on, in spite of any deterrent the law threw at them. On the 21st May 1910, Edward Hammond, Jim's son went out with Thomas Edwards from Bank Street on a wholesale fowl stealing spree of the local hen roosts. They stole nine fowls and one turkey from Mr. Sidney Wheway's property at the Shrubberies in Sutton Road valued at two pounds. They then stole five fowls belonging to Frederick Rowley from Beacon Street valued one pound. Finally they raided and stole four fowls from Edwin Cheadle in Beacon Street valued ten shillings.

At ten thirty on that night, Detective Thomas was making enquiries respecting some fowl thefts, when he saw the two men coming from Dark Lane, towards Eldon Street. He seized both men by the collars, but in the struggle that ensued Hammond got away and ran towards Tantarra Street. In a bag Hammond dropped, Detective Thomas found nine fowl. Edwards was taken to the police station and detained in the cells. At ten to twelve that night, Detective Thomas went to Hammond's home address in Eldon Street. The house contained about twenty or so known villains, including poachers and their wives. Edward Hammond was found skulking in bed feigning illness to avoid arrest. He said he was unwell and had been in bed for four hours, but Detective Thomas recognised him as the man who ran away.

On the Monday morning of the 23rd May, both men were brought up in front of the magistrates from the cells below, that included the Mayor, Councillor Williams. William Heap, a gardener employed by Mr. Wheway said he identified the birds at the police station as those which were missing from his pen. A boy named William Rowley from Beacon Street, said he saw two men sitting under a hedge with a brown lurcher dog walk away towards the Shrubberies. An hour later he saw the same men on top of Mr. Cheadle's pen. He went to tell his mother but on his return to the garden, saw them running away towards Dark Lane fields. Rowley identified Edwards as the man from Mr. Cheadle's fowl pen to the police while they were holding him in Chuckery Road that night. Another boy Frederick Sadler aged twelve, said he saw two men at the rear of houses in Beacon Street at one thirty on Saturday afternoon. They were sitting on a bank with a lurcher dog in Dark Lane. He saw one of the men send the dog to fetch one of the hens, which it did. The following morning he positively identified Hammond from among a number of other men as the offender. Sarah Cheadle, of 44 Beacon Street said she was missing three fowls from her pen.

Edwards told the court that he never had a dog, and that he did not go out in the afternoon. He was guilty of the first lot, but no more he said. The Chief Constable informed the bench that Edwards had not been convicted of theft since 1892, but Hammond appeared in

November 1908 for stealing a sweater. The Mayor said the bench found them both guilty of all three charges. The mayor said that he was determined to end fowl stealing once and for all in the town. Edwards who was forty-eight years old was sentenced to nine months and Hammond who was twenty-one, to six months both with hard labour. [218] [219]

Just to prove the old rogue had not yet hung up his nets, the king of poaching royalty was out again on Wednesday the 21st December 1910. Jim Hammond and his old mate Frederick Bond were seen by Police Constable Fisher in Mellish Road at twenty past six in the morning on a footpath leading to Calderfields. As he approached the men ran, but Bond was caught and had a bag containing three rabbits, netting and stakes. Hammond escaped but his identity was well known to the officer. Both men were summoned to court on the 3rd January 1911 charged with being in the unlawful possession of game. The bench comprised of Mr. Clare, Mr Lavender and Mr. Jagger. Constable Fisher told the court that the nets were wet and that the rabbits had been freshly caught because they were still not cold when he got to the police station. Bond admitted being in possession of the rabbits but denied they had come off the Calderfield's land. Hammond denied being there and said the officer was mistaken. Police Constable Fisher admitted that it was dark, but he could see well enough to identify him and he was unmistakably well-known. William Yates the owner of the property, said his land contained many rabbits and they were most likely his. Bond told the bench he had the wild rabbits off the turnpike road many miles away and the constable caught them on the way back. He said he needed the rabbits so that he could buy some new boots to make himself respectable. With a grin he said, "I am very sorry I was caught," which brought laughter to the courthouse. Mr. Lavender replied, "We are all sorry when we are caught, but we are not sorry until then, when it is too late". The chief constable, Alexander Thompson said their last convictions were at Lichfield in 1907 for night poaching where they were sentenced to three months hard labour. He said they often committed crimes together and both had numerous previous convictions for similar offences. The chief constable confirmed that Hammond was the head of the most notorious family in the district for poaching. Mr. Lavender enquired about previous convictions, "nothing for two years?" The chief constable said nothing he has been caught for! Bond asked the Bench to deal leniently with him and pleaded that this offence was not so bad as stealing fowl or geese, or anything like that. The old villains never knew when to be quiet, Bond said, "If I had done that, there would have been a stink," amid roars of laughter from the public. This was no doubt a reference to the sentences handed out to Edward, Jim's son the previous year. Mr. Lavender reminded him that he was in a court of law and advised him to say no more. Mr. Clare was obviously not amused by either defendant and before passing sentence said, "You think you are as entitled to the rabbits as the man who looks after them". Both received a fine of ten shillings and costs or fourteen days in prison. Mr. Clare concluded, you have both been dealt with very leniently this morning. I think that their age perhaps had something to do with the verdict. [220]

To round up what was going on in 1911, I will just summarise the family. My eldest son, William Henry was a carpenter living with his wife Margaret and their daughter Miriam in Weston Street. [221] Daughter Frances was cohabiting with my half-brother Edward Hammond at Fieldgate Terrace and they now had four children, Jack, Benjamin, Edward and James. [222] My daughter, Rose Lillian Smith lived with her husband Orlando in Western Road. Orlando was an engine stoker and they had five children living with them. [223] My other two sons, Enoch Edward and Arthur Ernest were both serving with the 1st Battalion of the South Staffordshire Regiment in Gibraltar. [224]

144

Abel, my younger brother was now sixty-five years old. He worked as an iron annealer and lived at Stammer's Yard with his wife Sophia. [225] His children from his first marriage had moved to the Birmingham area. Abel had five children living with him: William a tinner, twenty-one years; Enoch a tinner's assistant, nineteen years; Lily, seventeen an iron filer; May, fifteen an iron sorter and Alice, twelve who was still at school. Abel's eldest son John Thomas Reeves was a saddle tree riveter and lived with his wife Ada and their three children in Upper Brook Street. [226] His other son Abel, a tinner lived with his wife Henrietta and daughter Polly in Lower Foster Street. [227]

Jim Hammond was recorded as an iron moulder living with his wife Lucy at Eldon Street. [228] Living under the same roof was his son, Edward 'Ted' and his wife Susannah with their son, James Edward. Also living with Jim was his daughter, Nellie and his son, Enoch. His eldest daughter Eliza Record was living at Holtshill Lane, with her husband Charles and one daughter and three sons. [229] Thomas Benjamin Hammond alias James Hammond junior was living in Lower North Street with his wife Amelia and two children. [230]

By 1911 the face of the old Hammond gang was changing significantly. While poaching still went on, they were looking for easier ways to earn a dishonest living. Younger members of the family were beginning to take up the reins and slowly getting control of things. The business moved towards illegal betting and gaming which was far more profitable.

Matilda, Ben Hammond's widow was a forceful character to be reckoned with. She had four children, Eliza Margaret who was Ben's daughter, Edward Hammond, known as 'Big Ted,' Richard Thomas Hammond and Alfred Isaac Jones, nicknamed 'Pasha'. [231] [232] [233] [234] Eliza was a blood relative being my niece, the others all had different fathers as far as I knew. Matilda married a man called Robert Jones in 1890 and he bought the children up from youngsters. [235] Robert and

145

Matilda Jones were the elder partners in the 'new' betting business, with their children doing the running. Eliza Margaret married a man named Robert Phillips, an electro-plater who played a major part in the betting business with Big Ted Hammond. [236] Both the Phillips and the Jones families lived in Bank Street with Big Ted's round the corner in Bott Lane. [237] The need to enforce unpaid bets meant they had to have some muscle, so protection rackets and violence made an appearance in their repertoire. Not that the Hammond's were ever averse to giving defaulters a beating. The muscle for the team was provided by 'Big Ted' Hammond, Pasha Jones, and their cousin, Enoch Hammond, Jim's son. Their hard man reputations, were earned from backstreet scraps and from their pugilism in the boxing ring. To promote their reputations, they performed exhibition bouts in local pubs like the Spur Makers Arms in Tantarra Street and the Walsall Arms in Bank Street. The Walsall Arms was virtually ruled by the Hammond's who used it as their headquarters, a legacy started by Jim senior. So from all accounts it appeared that this was the new firm slowly taking over the Hammond gang activities.

As the criminal venture grew, so did the attention of the police to their activities. On the 2nd June 1911, Sergeant Cook saw one of the bookies runners making signals to Robert Phillips, who was taking bets in Ball Street. The runner Martin Cooley appeared at court and was given a four pounds fine, which he refused to pay preferring to do the month in prison instead. He also refused to name Phillips as the man taking the bets. [238]

Pasha Jones was fined four pound and costs on the 1st July 1911 for aiding and abetting Robert Phillips, who had only recently been fined for bookmaking. Police Constable Bell had seen Jones making signals to Phillips, so arrested him. Phillips came to his aid and threatened to assault the constable to assist Jones to escape. Only after the sternest warning from the constable who refused to back down did Phillips back

146

away. Fighting the law in broad daylight would have been a mistake even for the Hammond's. [239]

On the 3rd September 1911, Police Constable Sneyd saw a group of men betting on a game called Bank on a footpath in Brewood. The group consisted of John Rogers, Robert Phillips, John Carless, Edward Walters, Alfred Walters and Ernest Phillips all of Bank Street, together with James Hammond of Teddesley Street. Appearing at court on the 16th September 1911, they all pleaded guilty and received fines ranging from three to ten shillings with seven shillings costs each. [240]

With a string of incidents and numerous complaints it appeared Sergeant Cook was losing his patience with Robert Phillips, who always had loads of money, far more than he earned from his legitimate trade. To catch him, he set up two days of observations on the 5th and the 6th July 1912. He thought Phillips was bang at it, but couldn't believe his eyes at the extent. On the first day he saw one hundred and twenty men, two women and ten boys approach Phillips, out of which fifty-seven distinctly handed him slips. Phillip's constantly changed position making it hard to see, so there was probably many more exchanges. On day two he saw two hundred and thirty-two men and six boys go up to Phillips and eighty-five slips exchanged. Phillips was summoned to court on the 15th July for two offences of frequenting Bank Street for the purposes of illegal bookmaking or betting. At court the sergeant informed the bench that he saw a long line of men waiting, like the queue at the theatre. Several times he handed change over to customers and every now and then he passed things to his wife and mother-in-law through his own front door. He said he believed Phillips was conducting a tremendous trade. Phillip's pleaded guilty and had nothing to say, he had after all been well and truly caught. The court gave him a twenty pound fine or two months imprisonment. This was a very substantial sum of money in 1912 when the average annual wage for a fifty-six hour week was only one hundred and sixty pounds a year. [241]

Poaching was not gone completely however, some family habits die hard. On the 13th August 1913, Police Constable's Collins and Basson saw Ted Hammond, Jim's son, from Tantarra Street with his father-in-law, Harry Spink in Dark Lane. On seeing the officers they both made off on foot, but the officers gave chase and caught them in possession of thirteen rabbits. At court they claimed to have permission from the landowner to snare rabbits, but failed to provide any evidence. The Chief Constable said Spink was a very well known poacher with a list of previous convictions as long as his arm and Hammond had previous convictions for theft and aiding and abetting a bookmaker. Both were fined forty shillings with costs or twenty-one days imprisonment. [242]

That's a quick round up of the state of play back in the home town of Walsall, but meanwhile in Salt Lake there were things happening here to.

There was a massive theft of chopped wire from the Utah Copper Company over Christmas 1912, it was in all the papers. On the 2nd January 1913, Sheriff Sharpe gave my brother Enoch a visit at his foundry on South Sixth West Street and recovered some of the stolen property from the heist. Five suspects were soon arrested for the metal theft by the sheriff. Jack Wilson, Dan Grow, Ernest Grow (aka Irwin Groves), 'Curley' Arthur Curtis and James Buck, were part of an organised gang causing havoc across the county. They were also suspected of being involved in the Riverton Bank robbery job. Luckily for Enoch, Sheriff Sharpe had his sights set on gaoling the five, so was happy to use him as a witness against them. To be honest Enoch had no choice but to give evidence, the sheriff had him over a barrel. He could have thrown the book at him for receiving stolen goods and closed him down for good, had he refused to help convict the team. [243] [244]

148

In February 1914, I heard from England that Samual Proud one of the Hammond gang had been charged with attempted suicide after he tried to hang himself. He lost his mother and this sparked a downward spiral of events. He was remanded in custody for a fortnight, more for his own safety than anything else. At court he was released into the custody of his sister who offered him a good home. Life is so complex at times, you never know what goes on in the minds of others. [245] [246]

The year of 1914 was going to be dreadful, from start to finish. My daughter and her husband John Eaves moved away from Utah with their two daughters. John was a brakesman on the railroad and he went where the best offers of work were. I was rather looking forward to seeing the grandchildren growing up, so was sorry when they moved so far away, it saddened me greatly.

Then in April 1914, I had a bad accident at work while on nights as a watchman, minding a tractor engine at Thirteenth East and Fifth South Street. At six o'clock in the morning on the 15th April 1914, I finished my shift and was climbing down from the engine. I'm not sure how it happened, but I slipped and I fell cracking my side on the wheels of the huge machine. I knew I had done myself a serious mischief, being totally winded and struggling to breathe. Pushing seventy-one years of age, I was taken to the emergency hospital at police headquarters by Officer Armstrong. They found I had broken several ribs, which was horrendously painful and made it hard for me to breathe. It was Arbor Day and for years I had followed a tradition of planting three little trees. I did this no matter where I was in the world at the time. I got out the machine to check the roots of my trees, with the intention of planting them during the day, but then fell. My injuries were to be my reward, so this would be the first year I failed in my tradition. Officer Armstrong asked me what I was going to do about planting the trees, when I told him my story. I told him, I knew a little boy that lived next door and I was going to ask him to plant the trees for me. I had a great chat with the officer, who seemed fascinated by my life in the army and police, back in England. He said he thought I should write a book! [247]

Over the next few days I could hardly move, it had hurt me more than you can imagine. Pain is a very personal experience and this was bad. At one point I thought my time was up, but I battled through it. David acted as my nurse maid, the look he gave me made me realise I was an old man in an uncomfortable way. He told me I needed to slow down and for once he was right. I felt terribly battered but it was nothing in comparison to the darkness of the clouds forming over Europe. This evil storm was going to engulf the world in a way far blacker than my poor ribs. The gruesome evil was making its way throughout the summer like a dark smog towards the old country and would descend with a vengeance upon its people.

Chapter Eleven

The Evil of War

On the 4th August 1914, Britain declared war on Germany. The whole world took up arms because one man, Franz Ferdinand an Archduke was assassinated by a Bosnian Serb nationalist. This one death escalated into something unimaginable, which was going to shatter everybody's lives like a terracotta pot, never to be repaired. The grave news soon arrived in the United States, the home of a large number of ex-patriots from Great Britain. Utah was a very long way from Europe, but much of my family remained in Walsall. They were in the direct firing line of the war and it was closing in fast. I shuddered to think, the reality was all my sons in England had military experience and were of fighting age. All across Walsall and the rest of the country, young men were lining up to answer the call to arms. Walsall itself sent the best part of twenty-thousand men to fight and over two-thousand never returned to their families. Hundreds of others returned only a shadow of their former selves, horribly tainted and scarred by their experiences of war. Several came home with shrapnel and bullet wounds, mental illness or missing limbs and body parts.

The Walsall volunteers of the 5th Battalion of the South Staffordshire Regiment were recalled for duty. They paraded on the bridge on the 11th August before the mayor, Peter Bull for a civic send off. There were nine-hundred and fifteen men commanded by Lieutenant-Colonel Fiddian Green. Spirits must have been high but most of the poor souls were oblivious to what was coming their way. At the end of the parade and after the National Anthem played they marched off to Whittington barracks to the tune of 'Tommy Atkins'. [248]

Those young lads who enlisted, were loyal patriots prepared to make the ultimate sacrifice for their families at home. I think they genuinely believed they could get the job done quickly and be home for Christmas. A sense of duty and comradeship led them to sign up, but they had no idea what they were subscribing to. I don't think even the boys with military experience could have ever imagined just how terrible the war was going to be and exactly what they had to do to see it through. The sights, sounds and smells those boys must have endured meant that many would carry the horrors for the rest of their lives. My eldest son, William Henry and his two younger brothers, Enoch Edward and Arthur Ernest were all to serve in the South Staffordshire Regiment.

I saw some terrible things when I served, but the sheer firepower had advanced to a new level. This war was going to see men hiding in holes in the ground called trenches with a torrent of deafening artillery shells raining down at all times. Then, when the whistle blew they were to scale ladders into the firing line of indiscriminate but deadly German machine guns. Whilst running towards the enemy in some medieval fashion, lifelong friends were cut down, mutilated or blown up before their very eyes. The bodies of men and animals littered the desolated landscape destroyed by heavy bombardments from both sides. Poisonous and silent gas came in clouds to add to the relentless killing tools, removing even their ability to breathe fresh air.

To commemorate the service given by the lads of our family, I will give you the facts of the sacrifices they made. It's also worth taking a few minutes to remember the women and children left at home, unaware, but worried sick about what their fathers, brothers and sons were being subjected to. It was a time of terrible anticipation waiting for news from the western front. When men returned either on leave or with injuries in their hospital blues, they were not the same men. The dreaded telegram brought the chilling word of death and fear would follow the messenger as they came into your street.

152

My eldest, William Henry was a professional soldier for several years before the war. He served with the South Staffordshire Regiment and received a medal from the South African campaign. He was recalled for active service, on the day after war was declared, He was one of the first men sent to France with the British Expeditionary Force. Within the month he returned to England injured. He was back with the 1st Battalion in 1915. By March he was back in hospital with trench foot, caused by wading knee deep through trenches full of water and blood. [249] In June 1915, he received a crippling gunshot wound to his left ankle, forcing him to return to England injured and with a limp. [250] He walked with a stick after that and on the 1st December 1915 he was discharged from the army as unfit. Due to his pre-war service he had now completed his period of engagement. In total he had served thirteen years with the regiment. He had done more than his bit and was lucky to return with his life. He received the British War and Victory Medals and the 1914 Star with Clasp and Roses. [251]

My son, Arthur Ernest joined the South Staffordshire Regiment on 4th October 1905. He was only fifteen when he joined up and served for several years until he transferred to the reserve back at home. He worked at Walsall Railway Station for eighteen months after his return, until war broke out. He was recalled to the 2nd South Staffords and mobilised with the British Expeditionary Force on the 12th August 1914. Arthur was well known in Walsall and wrote many letters from the front to his friends and family. His letters described the grim conditions and he became one of the towns unpaid correspondents on the Western Front. His words were recounted in the local newspaper to graphically tell of the terrifying conditions. Before the war started Arthur frequented the Working Men's club in Station Street, with other railway workers near his place of work. In October 1914, he wrote a letter setting the scene of how things really were in the trenches. [252] [253] He described how on the 23rd August at the Battle of Mons, the regiment came under terrible fire from the Germans who battered their position with several shells. The South Staffords were first in the line when they went over the top. Arthur said, when the fun started, he grabbed hold of a crazed horse. The terrified creature was suddenly hit by an incoming shell, blowing it to bits right in front of him and covering him with its remains. Together with a comrade, he went out and found a wounded hussar with his arm hanging off. They carried him several miles to a village but he didn't survive. They were then ordered to hold the village from the German advance, ten times their number, in the hope of giving the villagers half a chance to evacuate. The battle that followed was hand to hand with fixed bayonets and the next day German bodies, numbering seven to eight hundred were piled up six feet high. After the fighting all the men were dead beat, but the joking and the kindness of the villagers kept them alive. He said about the German's, "They're Willies not fighters. They have only to see cold steel and they shout out, we're friends don't shoot." Soon afterwards the regiment was overrun and forced to get the hell out of there, bidding the Germans good-bye. His wartime humour led him to say, "I haven't had a shave or wash for ages, but I'm still the same as ever, waiting to post a leaden letter in a German, as a keepsake from Walsall." He ended by saying, shrapnel and shells were floating around all the time and he could catch one any minute. He said the money he earned was hoped to be spent with his friends at the club, so he hoped not to get hit. Arthur talked about 'Benny Blick,' a German shell, that made holes big enough to bury a house in, saying, "We don't half duck our nuts". [254] On one occasion the German's tricked them by sticking up a white flag and pretending to surrender. Then as they approached they opened fire from the flank. He said it would never happen again, because every German he came across was being sent "on a path of righteousness". This reminded me of what happed in China under the flag of truce when treachery prevailed. At the end of 1914, he told of his old friend Lance Corporal

Taylor from Walsall who had been killed. [255] [256] The Lance Corporal had served with both him and Enoch and his loss must have hit him hard. Arthur did return to Walsall on leave in the summer of 1915 and he married Eliza Webb on the 31st August 1915. She was a local Walsall girl who had been blind from birth. [257]

After the wedding Arthur returned to the Western Front and served at the Battle of the Somme on the 29th July 1916. Shortly afterwards his wife received the worst dreaded news at their home in West Bromwich Road. One of Arthur's officers wrote a personal letter to her saying, "He had been through some pretty tough times, but still remained one of the most trustworthy soldiers in the platoon. He was killed by a heavy shell while going up into the line, quite painlessly and apparently without a mark upon him. I am very sorry for you in your bereavement, as I know well that it is not we, who are in the thick of things, who suffer so much, as you, who are waiting at home. Your husband has died as a soldier, paying one part of the heavy price which must be paid, if we are to secure that victory which we hope is even now being won." Eliza also got a letter from a private of the King's Liverpool Regiment, who sent her various articles found in Arthur's possession. These included a Bible, photographs of his wife and niece, and an un-posted letter to Eliza. His sergeant wrote saying, "At all times he was bright and cheerful, and was popular with all whom he came in contact. As his platoon Sergeant, I knew him very well, and feel his loss keenly". He had served eleven years and five months with the colours. [258] [259] [260]

What can any father say at the death of a child, I should have been used to it. This was senseless madness and such a loss to the world. Out of our twelve children, six had died without a family of their own. At least Arthur was a man, a soldier and there was nothing I could have done to keep him safe. Nothing can be said or done after the sudden and tragic death of a relative, it hit me hard. I tried to hold my proudness of his service and sacrifice close to my heart, as a comfort for the devastating loss I felt. I was helpless and half a world away from Walsall. I'm only glad that Sarah was spared this tragic news, but I know they met again to walk together in eternal peace.

Arthur's brother, Enoch Edward originally joined the South Staffordshire Regiment on the 24th February 1905 and although he said he was eighteen, he was actually sixteen. He served before the war with Arthur all around the world, they were brothers and the best of mates. Enoch's military service meant he was time served and he could have left the army before the end of the war, having completed his period of engagement with the South Staffordshire Regiment. However, he re-enlisted with the Leicestershire Regiment and served until the 2nd April 1919. I don't think he ever got over the death of his brother and was determined to see the German's defeated if only to avenge Arthur's death. The war left an indelible stain on all our hearts, a mark that never faded by the passing of years.

Brother Abel's eldest son, John 'Jack' Thomas Reeves enlisted on the 6th August 1914 as a horse driver in the Army Service Corp. His pre-war service allowed him to be discharged on the 18th January 1916 having completed thirteen years service. He too re-enlisted in December 1916 and served a second period until finally being discharged in 1919. 261

These boys showed true grit, they knew the horrors of the front only too well. Nevertheless they were prepared to sacrifice all, rather than be at home while others took the fight. This was despite having enough service to qualify for a rest from the war.

Abel's younger son, Enoch Reeves became a gunner with the Royal Field Artillery and served from the 17th January 1916 until 31st March 1920. 262 I know that after the war he never spoke a word about the horrors and graphic scenes he witnessed. This was in part due to the fact that his wife, Harriet had lost her much loved brother Arthur Swann on the 17th February 1917, whilst serving with the South Staffordshire

Regiment [263]. Such was family tragedy that if it didn't get you one way, it got you another.

At the outbreak of war Ted Hammond, Jim's son was living with his wife, Susannah and three children in Bank Street, Walsall. On the 7th September 1914, Ted Hammond enlisted with the South Staffordshire Regiment at Walsall. He was working as a labourer at Thomas Evans and Sons, brass casters, at Summit Works. Ted was discharged as medically unfit due to chronic nephritis a kidney complaint. [264] Soon after he enlisted again in the Army Service Corp as a driver but was found out and discharged again as medically unfit. Undeterred he re-enlisted as a private with the 14th Battalion of the Hampshire Regiment. He served in France in the summer of 1916 and at Ypres in 1917. On the 26th June 1917, he was admitted to hospital with trench fever and stayed there until 1st July 1917. [265] Only a month later he was killed in action. Ted's case graphically illustrates the stigma attached to men being at home when their friends and family were away fighting abroad. Men felt compelled to keep rejoining, even when medically unfit to serve, some even used false names so the army had no record of any previous discharge history. [266] His wife Susannah received his personal effects amounting to two pounds, eight shillings and five pence and a war gratuity of nine pounds, ten shillings for her and their four fatherless children. [267]

My stepson Robert, often sent me the clipping from the local Walsall newspaper covering the war. One of which had a poem from Susannah to her dead husband Ted Hammond, 'Soldier, Asleep! Thy warfare o'er, Sleep the sleep that knows not breaking, Dream of battlefields no more, Days of danger, nights of waking'. [268] Susannah had already lost her brother, Harry Spink, who served before the war with Arthur and Enoch in Gibraltar. He was killed in action while stretcher bearing with the South Staffordshire Regiment on the 29th July 1916, exactly the same day as my boy, Arthur was killed. Having already taken one wounded comrade from the field, he was returning with another when hit by a German shell that instantly killed him. Susannah who lived in Bath Yard, Dudley Street had a letter from a comrade saying, "I am sorry to inform you that Harry was killed in action whilst doing his duty as a stretcher bearer. He had taken a wounded comrade down and was returning for another, when he was hit by a German shell, which killed him instantly, so it will perhaps be a consolation to you to know he suffered no pain." [269] The pain he was spared was now Susannah's to endure for a lifetime to come.

Robert's son Harry, who was named after me, joined the Royal Field Artillery on the 7th January 1915. He was discharged on the 15th August 1915, when they found out he was under the age and too young to enlist. [270] As soon as he was old enough he enlisted again and joined the Lincolnshire Regiment. The poor kid was killed in action on the 8th May 1918 and his body lies at Lille. [271] [272] This was crushing news to me, he was just a boy and was my grandson, his parents were distraught. His poor mother died a broken woman four years later at the age of forty-seven. I know that I went off to fight when I was young, but this made me appreciate the worry my mother must have felt for me.

Enoch Hammond, Jim's son, enlisted as a private in the South Staffordshire Regiment on the 20th October 1915. He was initially attached then compulsorily transferred to 10th Battalion of the Lincolnshire Regiment on the 10th July 1916. He was classified as missing in action on the 27th April 1918. He had in fact been captured by the German's, news came through on the 12th June 1918 that he was a prisoner of war. He was repatriated after the end of the war on the 2nd December 1918 and discharged from the army on the 23rd February 1919. [273]

As for Matilda Ruff's sons, they had to take a break from the rackets being run in Walsall. To be fair their crooked dealings in Walsall did not stop them serving their country well, when the calling came.

Edward 'Big Ted' Hammond was a gunner and fought with the Royal Garrison Artillery. He was promoted to corporal on the 11th April 1918 and served until 12th September 1919. [274] His two half-brothers also served King and Country, Richard Thomas Hammond with the South Staffordshire Regiment and Alfred 'Pasha' Jones with the Grenadier Guards. Alfred was awarded the Military Medal by the King for bravery in the field in 1918.[275]

Even in the United States there was no good news to be reported. On 27th December 1916, my brother Enoch died from diabetes in Salt Lake City aged sixty-seven years. [276] He was not in great shape either physically or mentally. He had been having marriage and money problems and had spiralled down to a dark place, where he was out of reach. [277] Nonetheless, I was terribly shaken by the unexpected news of his death in amongst the rest of the trauma going on in the world. I had not only lost a brother, but a very old lifelong friend. He was after all the main reason I had come to live in America. He was buried following a Mormon service on the last day of the year 1916. His funeral at the city cemetery was such a sad old affair, especially after the recent separation from Mary Jane after forty-one years of marriage. It was a cold and miserable Sunday afternoon and awkward due to the breakup, but thats life, or death in this case.[278]

My youngest son David, lived with me in Salt Lake City beyond the jurisdiction of being called by the British military. Initially the United States remained neutral in the war, but German attacks on shipping continued to increase. They hit several passenger liners resulting in the death's of many United States citizens. Pressure was on the establishment to protect their people at sea and on the 6th April 1917, President Wilson declared war on Germany. He said the Americans were being forced to enter the war, in order to make the world safe for democracy. David was called up for military service on the 29th May 1917, when his conscription came through. He appealed for exemption on the grounds of being the only support of an aged father, me! [279] He asked the board to consider that, I had one son fighting with the English forces in France and had lost another at the Battle of the Somme. The appeal was unsuccessful and he was called up for military service on the 2nd October 1917. [280] Having been at my side for so long, I struggled without him. I was forced to realise for the first time, just how much help I really needed. It seemed like overnight, I had become an old and vulnerable human being.

David commenced his military service on the 23rd October 1917 as a private in the 145 Field Artillery. He was stationed at Camp Kearny, San Diego County, California along way from home. On the 3rd June 1918, David seized the opportunity to apply for naturalisation and full citizenship of the United States. [281] His military service no doubt assisted him to achieve this and he became a real American.

David was discharged from the army on the 28th February 1919. He did not see any active service like his brothers, but I think it had matured him into a fine young man. When David returned I was seventy-six and was more or less dependant on him. Although mobile and reasonably well, my working days were well and truly over. A lifetime of physical work and fighting my corner had taken its toll on every one of my joints. The days of getting new body parts were still way in the future, the old fashioned way was to suffer. Each day brought new challenges and David returned to work as a clerk for the Denver and Rio Grand Railroad Company to support us both.

Fresh from being discharged from the army, my son Enoch returned home to the streets of Walsall. Life in the old town was never the same again and there was a sombre atmosphere. Men, woman and children had all been touched by the travesty of war and the trauma remained on their faces and in their minds for years afterwards. He found his brothers blind and vulnerable widow Eliza, devastated by the death of her husband. Enoch was a kind and considerate lad and wanted to do

160

the right thing after all the heartache. I remember how me and Sarah had to weather our own emotional storms before we got together. They too were bound by mutual grief and reached out to each other to fill the emotional void left by Arthur's death. The two were married at Walsall Registry Office on the 26th July 1919. 282 It was actually unlawful for them to marry until the introduction of the Deceased Brother's Widow's Marriage Act in 1921. The law was stupid and controversial, you could not marry your widowed sister-in-law, but since 1907 you could marry your dead wife's sister. It was all a bit of a nonsense really and many of these marriages took place after the war with the clergy turning a blind eye. After all there was a shortage of good men, the best part of a whole generation had been wiped out by that evil war.

In the spring of 1920, I had to concede to myself that David would never settle down and marry so long as he had me like a mill stone hanging around his neck. He was only ever going to do what was right by me, so that left me with a decision to make. I had come to the realisation that my time was running out, so what did I want? I did not want to burden David anymore and I really wanted to see my grandchildren after the brutal losses of the war. My daughter Annie lived at Riverbank, California, which was quite a distance away from Salt Lake. She was settled in a stable home, with her husband and four children. She knew David was at work all day, while I was struggling and wrote to ask me if I wanted to go and live with her. To be perfectly honest, I needed all the help I could get. This really was my last chance saloon to get some comfort in my final years and I would have been a fool to pass it by. I had not seen my daughter for a while, so I was happy to up sticks and accept her offer of help. When I told David my plans he looked quite sad about me leaving. I suppose my departing left him abandoned alone, with his family scattered to the four winds. I brought him to this foreign land, but he now had his chance to build his own family and he was a proper American now! Deep down I'm sure he realised I was doing him a favour and giving him an opportunity to move on with his own life. I just knew it was the right thing to do.

It was a days travelling to Riverbank and god I had forgotten how tiring it was going on a long journey. Getting to California took it out of me, but my daughter thankfully met me at the station. She was all grown up, almost twenty-four years old and looked well. When I first saw her, it was like looking at my Sarah. It felt so much like Sarah had called me here to take care of me and I was comforted by her apparition in the face of our daughter. Annie had four children, three girls, Marie, Marguerite and Byra and a boy, Lloyd and it was great to see them all. We got together that night for a family meal my son-in-law, John at home from work. Their house was a nice property in High Street, a wide residential street with mainly single storey houses. Seeing the kids was a real tonic, I missed being part of a family and it brightened my mood. The decision to come to Riverbank was right for me and for what ever time I had left. Spring was in the air and everything was good. A feeling of contentment blew through my remaining few white locks. The children had put a smile on my face and seeing my daughter settled was the most pleasing of blessings. All those worries when she was growing up, it all turned out for the best. My mind flashed back to that horrible night she went missing and the dread I felt until she was found safe.

Riverbank was a good move for me, enjoying my grandchildren and meeting new friends. The grandchildren loved hearing all the stories and tales about my adventures and times gone by. They listened to my ramblings wide eyed and in awe of every word I said. It was such a wonderful time with those fantastic little people.

Like all things, nothing can last for ever and my health began to take a nose dive by the end of 1921. I had one or two worrying falls and after each one I became more frail. In spring 1922, I was taken to Modesto hospital after becoming very unsteady and light headed. They examined me and decided to keep me in hospital for my own safety. I needed round the clock care and frankly my body slowly gave up the will to carry me anywhere under its own steam. I remained in a bed bound condition at hospital, each day my body became weaker and weaker. I held on to what was left of my dignity by staying compos mentis, so was thankful for that small mercy. I knew my body could no longer to do anything my mind told it to. I also knew it would not be long before things gave up all together.

On the 2nd April 1923 my niece Marie, Enoch's daughter died of kidney disease in Los Angeles, she was just forty-nine years old, it was so sad to hear the news of her passing. [283]

On the following morning of Tuesday 3rd April 1923, I heard the nurse bringing the drinks around for the daily wake up call. I looked out of the window and a bright blade of light hit the back of my eyes. This was no normal day and no usual light. Blinded, my arms dropped to my sides and my body and speech was paralysed. I realised straight away I was gone and my physical time on this planet was over. Within a couple of minutes all that I knew to be real had gone, my time was up. I looked down at the haggard old carcass on the bed, it reminded me of the crusty old leftover shell of a caterpillar chrysalis. It was abandoned after the life within had fluttered away, now devoid of any useful purpose. Like the butterfly, I was now free to leave and travel to the next place, my metamorphosis was complete. That skeletal shell of my mortal self was removed by the Oakdale Undertaking Company. They boxed it up neatly in a wooden coffin for its final journey. My funeral was on the following day at the funeral parlour of Johns and Woods in Oakdale. My family and a few friends and acquaintances attended the low key service and some kind words were uttered to commemorate my demise. The coffin was taken to the Oakdale Citizens Cemetery, where the Reverend Hugh Baker said a few final words of goodbye at the graveyard. At every funeral I had ever attended, I always thought that this day would at some time come, the day I returned to my loved ones. I was not wrong! My box was slowly and carefully lowered into the ground towards the bottom of the purpose made pit dug just for it. As my few family members stood throwing soil on top of the lid, I realised none of my story had really been told. I had taken the bulk of my life story to the grave with me. While the gravedigger rested from filling up the void in the ground, a Mourning Cloak butterfly landed on the handle of his spade. Having spread its wings for a few short seconds the butterfly was gone. My life span was over in a flutter of the butterfly's wings. The grave was completely refilled before long, leaving just a small mound of earth as a reminder. [284]

Over just a few short years, the rest of my living relatives were gone. Half-brother Edward died aged sixty-two in 1924, leaving my daughter Frances a widow aged forty-four. [285] He was followed by my youngest brother Abel in 1931 who died at the Manor hospital, Walsall. [286] Alfred Reeves my nephew, son of Enoch passed in California in 1936, while working at one of the big film studios. [287] My son Enoch Edward died in Walsall in 1936, aged forty-eight, so young, but the war had reduced the years of many men that survived its horrors. [288] David did eventually marry in 1924 to a divorced woman named Lottie. [289] She had a son from her first marriage who David bought up, just like I had done with Robert. They had two daughters, Dorothy and Emma. David died in Salt Lake in 1938 at the age of forty-six from a sudden heart attack. Seems like the Reeves family is not without its genetic fault line. [290] My daughter Frances died in 1939 followed by her sister Rose Lilian in 1940. [291] [292] The old rogue Jim Hammond almost managed to out live us all, dying at Walsall in 1945 aged 91 years. [293] So the saying, 'Only the Good Die Young,' may be right after all. The following year in 1946 my last and eldest son, William Henry died aged sixty-eight years. [294] My adopted son Robert Stanton outlived all his half siblings and died at Walsall at the end of 1949 aged seventy-four years. [295]

My living memory was all but gone like a shadow with the passing of the sun. Suddenly there was nobody left who knew me in life, all trace of my existence had been blown away like an autumn leaf falling in a strong autumn wind.

A great thought evoking thing is, why out of all those children who died in infancy and men who died in war was I chosen to survive to a ripe old age. I had been granted a long and adventurous life, while others were snuffed out before they even began. There must be a reason, life really is a lottery. Maybe genetics and making the right decisions helps, but you can't help but think there is a higher force at play.

Chapter Twelve

The Great Escape

S o it all ended for me on the 3rd April 1923, when finally something called arteriosclerosis finished me off. That's the medical term for hardening of the arteries caused by the effects of old age. Basically the blood flow slows down until eventually it stops being viable for life to continue. To be fair, I was almost eighty years old and had managed to pack a load into the time I had been given. The bible teaches that men should expect to live on earth for three score years and ten, that's seventy years. So I did all right and can't really complain, all in all. But life is never long enough for an enquiring and adventurous mind. There is always something you just want to do or finish when your end comes. When my life ended I believed there was so much more to do.

Most of all, I desperately wanted my story to live on. I wanted people to remember me! How after my death could I ever possibly achieve being remembered. I'm not stupid enough to ever think I could physically rise from my cold grave inside the gates of Oakdale Citizens Cemetery, California. The human body really is mortal and after death, returns to the dust from whence it came. I remember the teachings of Sunday school - Ecclesiastes 12:7 - And the dust returns to the earth as it was, and the spirit returns to God who gave it. Nothing of a material nature remains of me among the rows of old grave stones. Even the cemetery officials can't be exactly sure where I rest in peace, other than that I'm buried somewhere in row four. Family members stopped visiting my grave decades ago and there has been no flowers decorating the earth for such a long time. I know a few virtual flowers have been left more recently but nothing for real. It just leaves you thinking what life is all about. Had I become just another forgotten, uncelebrated and all but unremembered name in the ground of a foreign land. My body lies five-thousand two-hundred miles from my home town, but my soul is frustrated and desperate to tell my story. Just before I died, I dreamed of going home to Walsall one last time, but it was not to be.

They say you never die while you remain in the minds of the living, so maybe there was hope for me. It is not as easy as it sounds, how could I possibly be remembered by the living? The human soul unlike the weak body is indestructible. With hunger, the soul continues to want remembrance and to be rekindled in the hearts of living relatives. Years ago rich people paid priests to pray for their souls after they had died so this is nothing new. The spirit goes on and on and I was eager to find a way back to my family once again, if only for a short time. After almost one hundred years of being away from my mortal life, I have many new descendants around the world. In some small way, I desperately wanted to remain a memory to some of them. It's comforting to be remembered, it is part of human nature, even when you are alive and kicking. There is a time in everyone's life that you ponder how your memory will live on in the hearts of your loved ones after you have gone. Immortality is defined by being remembered, whats wrong with that?

Whether you have worldly rags or riches, life is all about the stories that you create. What really counts are the memories of family and friends you make during your lifetime. Even better I thought, if my memories can touch the lives of family and friends who never knew me at all. I wanted to be formally introduced to them from the pages of a book. By now you are probably all wondering what this last chapter is all about. How could I write my own life story after all these years. I did not leave any diaries or journals about my travels to make the way for this book.

I needed to find someone to be my storyteller, someone who could pick up the trail, left during my time on earth. Someone to recognise the track of my footprints pressed into the sands of time. It had to be a blood relative, but finding one with the special attributes is not so simple. Look around your own family, who would you trust with such a task? An author would only come along once in a generation or so. But years of perseverance was to pay off when the great grandson of my brother arrived in the sights of my objective to be resurrected. I had at last found a possible narrator. It only remained for my spirit to lead him to the signposts of the past and discover the facts of my life. I had to convince my would be voice-over, to tell things the way I wanted them to be told. The challenge had begun, I just had to creep into the minds eye of my chosen one and guide them to present my life in words on the pages of a book.

What the heck am I talking about you say, the story has been good up to here, but read on! That's why I insisted the odd part of my story was put at the back of the book, so as not to put off the conservative historians. I know there will be many sceptics and disbelievers, I'm fully prepared for that. To be honest other peoples opinions are not important to this work, what's important are the words on the page. To explain how I achieved this feat of escapology and break from obscurity, I will try to explain the workings involved. Just like directing people in thick fog, sometimes the way through is clouded and may be a little clumsy.

Most people will have heard of something called a family tree, it illustrates a persons lineage, showing mothers and fathers from past generations. Pretty simple stuff, they have been about for years, but were mainly the preserve of the nobility or the pretentious. In recent times, people have become more and more curious about their own origins. Who were the people from the past who breathed life into us and whose blood flows within our veins. It's called genealogy, the study of families and the tracing of lines.

I have already mentioned my fascination for growing trees, something I did all throughout my life. Trees are great for so many reasons, especially wildlife and the environment. Animals such as squirrels and birds build their homes and playgrounds in trees and who doesn't like a treehouse. It is widely known that trees actually produce oxygen, the very thing that allows human life to breathe. Like human life, some trees change with the seasons and each year is recorded in the rings that forms within its inner core. These rings like the generations of man show the passing of years, each one intrinsically linked to each other. This is very similar to the way that human generations are linked, with the new ones living and breathing on the outside and the older ones locked within. Each autumn, dead leaves fall to the ground to return to dust. In spring new ones grow and by summer the seeds appear to bring a new tree to the world.

Like the rings of a tree, the human form passes on a record of past life from parent to child. Every human has twenty-three pairs of chromosomes inherited from their parents. I'm no scientist, so to be simple deoxyribonucleic acid, DNA for short is the building block of life. It is the hereditary fibre, the unique code that defines your very being. Segments of DNA get passed down through several generations to you and many others who share your ancestors. This may sound like elaborate science, but it's well known that people from the same family are similar to each other and sometimes have the same character traits. That's why the words familiar and family are the same thing. I am going to tell you my theory, so brace yourself.

I believe that locked within the deoxyribonucleic acid, is a memory gene, an echo, a shadow from the past. When conditions are right memories can be carried through the blood and relayed to the minds eye of relatives living further down the line and into the future. You may

169

think this is madness, but think hard, can any of this be credible? These flashes of memory can come in dreams and in subconscious moments making them hard to decipher.

Throughout the centuries there have been stories told of ghostly visitations from the past and all kinds of other supernatural occurrences. People are fascinated by spooky folklore and tales about haunted happenings. Many hours are spent wondering and debating and picking through the shreds of truth in the phenomenon. Mediums and spiritualists, tell of the afterlife and claim they have messages from those who have passed to the other side. There is one thing for sure, no living person can tell you what happens to your spiritual presence when you die, including priests and scientists. The facts are, most of the established religions teach their followers about the afterlife, heaven and hell, good and evil. So I say, believe whatever you want, but plenty go to the other side believing in life after death. The ancient Egyptians built huge pyramids filled with treasure to send their pharaohs to the next world. Everyone has heard of angels, a spiritual presence bringing messages from God in heaven, back down to earth. Guardian angels are sent to protect their own, they influence their lives and keep them safe. There are whole cultures that worship their ancestors, I'm not telling you anything new, just something you may not have considered seriously. There has to be life after death, right!

Thankfully my chronicler, was 'touched by my falling leaf'. He heard my soft whisperings coming from the void between the afterworld and the land of the living. My leaf fell from our family tree in 1923, it slowly fluttered down brushing against the brow of my kinsman to settle at his desk. The semaphore of light I transmitted, formed the pictures and sounds he picked up and interpreted. This contact was my message from bardo, my words from the grave. This serendipity spoke to him and the story began. The unexplainable thoughts he received without reason, came with a strange essence of truth. The French word 'déjà vu' is what I'm talking about, that overwhelming feeling that you have seen it all before. He saw things I had seen, but was reluctant to believe them as true. Have you ever heard of someone who has inexplicably dreamed about something from the past. Hearing the words from a departed loved one, or felt their presence, it's hard to accept as real. I locked on to my man when he started researching the family history about thirty years ago. It was obvious then that nobody knew much about the family, I had a great deal of work to do. Luckily major advancements in technology came to my aid, with a world wide library of records opening up to the fingertips.

In 1994 a family death led to the discovery of a dusty sepia picture of an old man with a beard. That haunting anonymous picture was me! It almost hypnotised my man, who I caught staring at the picture in a trance. That was my lure to bring him into my plan, he was both fascinated and mesmerised. I managed to subconsciously pass my instructions to him, bringing down the 'brick walls' that were preventing my name being placed on the family tree. Once I saw my youngest brother Abel appear, I knew I was just a few steps from coming home. When Henry Reeves appeared on the page, I was finally back. I now only needed to add the meat on the bones of my life story.

I painstakingly watched over him making sure that every tap of the keyboard formed the words on his screen, just as if my own quill was writing them. The ink from my metaphoric pen formed the words that he wrote, flowing like the familiar deoxyribonucleic acid through our veins. Word by word, sentence by sentence, page by page, my umbra began to walk again, retracing my footsteps in the dust of time. Of course my life had interesting features and there were similarities between us that drew him in. When he realised we both of had worked for the police on the same streets in Walsall, I had him hooked. With his inquisitive detective mind, he was locked like a terrier on my case. I knew he was never going to let go until he found me out, I could not shake his tenacity off. I was delighted by his careful reconstruction of the documents he found. They were placed together like a jigsaw, to paint the picture depicting my life. He knitted all the facts together like a file for court, which read like my autobiography. He tried to write it as an assembly of historical facts, but I insisted he did it my way. It is fair to say, I watched him struggle with the concept of this essentially being a ghost story. He was certainly a hard nut to crack, as he was no believer at first. I watched his hectic life unfold and he too had many tragedies and gruesome ordeals to deal with along the way. I stood at his side in times of trouble to guide a path whenever I could. I had to protect my investment and the man I hoped to breathe life back into my memory.

The opportunity to write my words was constantly interrupted when life got in the way. It stopped and started, I realised this was a marathon not a sprint in terms of getting things completed. When he retired from the police in 2016, I really thought we were on the verge of being finished. This was thwarted when his dear mum was diagnosed with vascular dementia. I accepted without question that he had to look after her and I can't blame him for that. Duty and responsibility was a family trait and something I wholeheartedly subscribed to. Unfortunately this quality skipped a few family members, too wrapped up in themselves to bother. I'm sure that some people never see their image reflected back in the mirror!

It was a great blow when Catherine passed in 2020 after a valiant battle with dementia aged ninety years. She had inspired him to look at family history and she was the one that nurtured his interest. She always believed in the afterlife and often referred to relatives from the past as still being present. She spoke to them, to help her get through the day and she never lost her faith until dementia stole it from her. She literally fought to keep it to the very end. Her sad death meant it was almost time to get my story done.

I now present my greatest achievement of all, my story. Rising like a phoenix to the pages of this book, I hope you enjoy. Unearthed from the dusty old documents dug out with archeological precision and presented from the hidden clues by my modern day detective.

His grandfather Enoch, was the young nephew who in 1908, said I might come back one day, he was right and that's in some way thanks to him.

I would like to thank you all for reading my story and breathing life back into my memory. Believe as much as you will, don't blame anyone but me for mistakes, we all make them. I would also just say to all the family historians and tree builders out there, "It's ok to see dead people, we are very addictive and persuasive". Till we meet again, Henry Reeves (1843-1923).

I dedicate this book to my great grand nephew, Paul Reeves the man I managed to persuade to listen to my story! I hope he achieves as good a reward as me. Henry R.

Revelation 1:17b - 18a: "Don't be afraid! I am the First and Last. I am the living one. I died, but look – I am alive forever and ever!"

About the Author

Paul Reeves was born in the early 1960's in Walsall Wood, Staffordshire. He attended both Walsall Wood County Primary and Shire Oak Schools. The second child of five sons, he was born and brought up on a council estate near the local colliery. In 1986 he joined West Midlands Police as a uniform constable. He retired after thirty years in 2016 with an exemplary character at the rank of Detective Sergeant. Most of his service was as a detective investigating serious crimes, burglary, robbery, assaults and murder. He also dealt with serious and organised crime utilising a range of specialist policing techniques. Towards the later years of his career he returned to Bloxwich and Walsall carrying out both force and local criminal investigations. Paul now takes things easy and enjoys his family time with grandchildren and holidays away. Having seen the worst of humankind, it is nice to step back and allow the scars of thirty years policing to slowly fade.

Dedication

Paul dedicates his work to his mother Catherine Worley who taught him right from wrong and was the driving force behind looking at the past. She will always be remembered. Catherine Worley-Reeves (1930-2020) - Paul R.

Acknowledgments

To complete a book such as this takes a great deal of time and effort and without the help of others would be all but impossible. My mother was a great inspiration for our family history and helped along the way with interest and encouragement. I also have to say thanks to my long suffering wife Paula, for patiently letting me work at this research sometimes at the expense of valuable family time. It was never easy to understand the talking to dead people part. For proofreading I thank my daughter Emily and sister Jenny (Paula's sister) who I kind of forced into reading my ramblings. Appreciation goes to several fellow genealogists who I have been in contact with over the many years of research. I thank especially the ones who waited for me, when others thought this book was a pipe dream. For the title, I thank an old colleague Phil C, who used 'Remember Me' as a catchphrase when he knocked peoples doors. To all the funny and fascinating people past and present, I say thanks. Also to any friends and former colleagues, you all helped make the unique, quirky, but well formed character that I am today. I know for some my acquired taste was too much and to those I have nothing to send but best wishes. To anyone that I have inadvertently missed, sorry, its a sign of my age.

Further Reading

1) From Calcutta to Pekin by John Hart Dunne, Captain Ninty Ninth Regiment, published London by Samson Low, Son, and Co., 1861

2) Incidents in the China War of 1860 compiled from the private journals of General Sir Hope Grant G.C.B. Commander of the English Expedition by Henry Knollys. Published by William Blackwood and Sons 1875.

3) Narrative of the North China Campaign of 1860 by Robert Swinhoe, published by Smith, Elder and Co., 1861.

4) A Memoir of Lieutenant-General Sir Garnet J. Wolseley by Charles Rathbone Low published by Richard Bentley and Son 1878.

5) Sister Dora, A Biography by Margaret Lonsdale by Roberts Brothers, 1890.

I have used numerous websites during the course of this work in order to verify the factual information. The major sites include ancestry, findmypast, familysearch, British Newspaper Archive, CWGC, freeBMD and GRO to name but a few.

[1] England, Births and Christenings, 1538-1975. Salt Lake City, Utah: FamilySearch, 2013. FHL Film Number:1999481 Reference ID:13

[2] England, Births and Christenings, 1538-1975. Salt Lake City, Utah: FamilySearch, 2013. FHL Film Number - 426520

[3] England, Births and Christenings, 1538-1975. Salt Lake City, Utah: FamilySearch, 2013. FHL Film Number - 421590

[4] General Register Office. England and Wales Civil Registration Indexes. London, England: Benjamin HAMMOND married Margaret REEVES at Aston, Birmingham in Q4/1853 (Volume 6d, Page 374)

[5] England, Marriages, 1538–1973. Salt Lake City, Utah: FamilySearch, 2013. FHL Film Number:1470945, Reference ID:p84 n252

[6] General Register Office. England and Wales Civil Registration Indexes. London, England: Margaret HALFPENNY died aged 88 years at Stone Q1/1890 (Volume 6b, Page 20)

[7] General Register Office. England and Wales Civil Registration Indexes. London, England: Thomas HALFPENNY died aged 76 years at Stone Q1/1873 (Volume 6b, Page 26)

[8] England, Marriages, 1538–1973. Salt Lake City, Utah: FamilySearch, 2013. FHL Film Number: 0873646 IT 3, 435871, 435872, 435873, 435874

[9] General Register Office. England and Wales Civil Registration Indexes. London, England: William REEVES born Aston Q4/1837 (Volume 16, Page 170). Mothers maiden name HIGGINSON.

[10] General Register Office. England and Wales Civil Registration Indexes. London, England: Sarah REEVES born Burton Upon Trent Q4/1839 (Volume 17, Page 7). Mothers maiden name HALFPENNY.

[11] Census Returns of England and Wales, 1841. Class: HO107; Piece: 1149; Book: 8; Civil Parish: Aston; County: Warwickshire; Enumeration District: 27; Folio: 31; Page: 16; Line: 5; GSU roll: 464184

[12] General Register Office. England and Wales Civil Registration Indexes. London, England: Thomas Edward REEVES was born Aston Q2/1841 (Volume 16, Page 200). Mothers name EGGINSON.

[13] General Register Office. England and Wales Civil Registration Indexes. London, England: Thomas Edward REEVES died Aston Q4/1842 (Volume 16, Page 141)

[14] Birmingham Church of England Burials, Library of Birmingham. Reference Number: DRO 41; Archive Roll: M94

[15] England Roman Catholic Parish Baptisms, Birmingham Archdiocesan Archives Page 13

[16] General Register Office. England and Wales Civil Registration Indexes. London, England: Peter REEVES born Walsall Q4/1845 (Volume 17, Page 228). Mothers name HIGGINSON.

[17] General Register Office. England and Wales Civil Registration Indexes. London, England: Peter REEVES died Walsall Q1/1846 (Volume 17, Page 183)

[18] General Register Office. England and Wales Civil Registration Indexes. London, England: George Henry REEVES born Walsall Q2/1847 (Volume 17, Page 269). Mothers name HIGGINSON

[19] General Register Office. England and Wales Civil Registration Indexes. London, England: Henry George REEVES died at Walsall Q3/1849 (Volume 17, Page 193)

[20] General Register Office. England and Wales Civil Registration Indexes. London, England: Enoch REEVES born Walsall Q4/1849 (Volume 17, Page 248). Mothers name HIGGINSON.

[21] Census Returns of England and Wales, 1851: Class: HO107; Piece: 2023; Folio: 521; Page: 63; GSU roll: 87428-87429

[22] Census Returns of England and Wales, 1851: Class: HO107; Piece: 2023; Folio: 43; Page: 14; GSU roll: 87428-87429

[23] Birmingham, England, Church of England Marriages and Banns, 1754-1937. Reference Number: DRO 41; Archive Roll: M88

[24] General Register Office. England and Wales Civil Registration Indexes. London, England: Benjamin HAMMOND born Walsall Q4/1854 (Volume 6b, Page 455). Mothers name HIGGINSON

[25] General Register Office. England and Wales Civil Registration Indexes. London, England: James HAMMOND born Walsall Q2/1856 (Volume 6b, Page 577). Mothers name HIGGINSON

[26] General Register Office. England and Wales Civil Registration Indexes. London, England: George HAMMONDS born Walsall Q3/1859 (Volume 6b, Page 542). Mothers name HIGGINSON

[27] General Register Office. England and Wales Civil Registration Indexes. London, England: Edward HAMMONDS born Walsall Q4/1861 (Volume 6b, Page 520). Mothers name HIGGISON

[28] General Register Office. England and Wales Civil Registration Indexes. London, England: George HAMMOND died Walsall Q1/1861 (Volume 6b, Page 366)

[29] General Register Office. England and Wales Civil Registration Indexes. London, England: William O TOOL/REEVES was born Walsall Q2/1858 (Volume 6b, Page 576).

[30] British Army Service Records 1760-1915 - Chelsea Pensioners' discharge documents 1760-1887 - WO121. Box 0227 1872.

[31] In 2021 this would equate to a tidy sum of about five-hundred pounds

[32] Census Returns of England and Wales, 1861. Class: RG 9; Piece: 2017; Folio: 11; Page: 19; GSU roll: 542903

[33] General Register Office. England and Wales Civil Registration Indexes. London, England: Thomas BULLERS married Sarah REEVES at Aston Q4/1861 (Volume 6d, Page 353)

[34] Kerry Evening Post: 16 November 1864, Page 3

[35] Hampshire Independent: 8 November 1865, Page 4

[36] Alnwick Mercury: 13 February 1869, Page 3

[37] Cardiff Times: 13 February 1869, Page 7

[38] Hampshire Telegraph: 2 October 1869, Page 4

[39] Hampshire Telegraph: 2 October 1869, Page 8

[40] Henley Advertiser: 12 August 1869, Page 5

[41] Aldershot Military Gazette: 6 July 1872, Page 6

[42] Hampshire Advertiser: 14 September 1872, Page 7

[43] Aldershot Military Gazette: 14 September 1872, Page 3

44 Census Returns of England and Wales, 1871. Class: RG10; Piece: 2960; Folio: 115; Page: 21; GSU roll: 836427

45 Census Returns of England and Wales, 1871. Class: RG10; Piece: 2965; Folio: 27; Page: 13; GSU roll: 836429

46 General Register Office. England and Wales Civil Registration Indexes. London, England: Abel REEVES married Emma BIRD in Walsall Q4/1872 (Volume 6b, Page 1082)

47 General Register Office. England and Wales Civil Registration Indexes. London, England: Henry REEVES married Elizabeth SHARRATT at Aston Q1/1873 (Volume 6d, Page 310)

48 Birmingham Church of England Marriages and Banns, 1754-1937. Reference Number: DRO 41; Archive Roll: M92

49 General Register Office. England and Wales Civil Registration Indexes. London, England: Enoch REEVES married Mary Jane CARPENTER at Walsall Q3/1873 (Volume 6b, Page 902)

50 Walsall Free Press and General Advertiser - 6 September 1873, Page 4

51 General Register Office. England and Wales Civil Registration Indexes. London, England: John STANTON married Sarah HAWLEY at Stafford Q3/1874 (Volume 6b, Page 4)

52 Birmingham Daily Post, 19 January 1875, Page 8.

53 Birmingham Daily Post, 10 March 1875, Page 8

54 General Register Office. England and Wales Civil Registration Indexes. London, England: Elizabeth REEVES aged 24 years died at Walsall Q2/1875 (Volume 6b, Page 409)

55 General Register Office. England and Wales Civil Registration Indexes. London, England: Robert STANTON born Walsall Q3/1875 (Volume 6b, Page 675). Mothers name HAWLEY.

56 General Register Office. England and Wales Civil Registration Indexes. London, England: Robert HAWLEY died aged 60 years at Walsall Q4/1875 (Volume 6b, Page 394)

57 Walsall Observer and South Staffordshire Chronicle: 16 October 1875, Page 2

⁵⁸ General Register Office. England and Wales Civil Registration Indexes. London, England: Henry REEVES married Sarah STANTON at Walsall Q4/1876 (Volume 6b, Page 1037)

⁵⁹ Walsall Observer and South Staffordshire Chronicle: 19 May 1877, Page 3

⁶⁰ General Register Office. England and Wales Civil Registration Indexes. London, England: William Henry REEVES was born in Walsall Q1/1878 (Volume 6b, Page 704). Mothers name STANTON.

⁶¹ Birmingham Daily Post: 24 April 1878, Page 8

⁶² Wolverhampton Express and Star: 24 April 1878, Page 2

⁶³ Walsall Observer and South Staffordshire Chronicle: 27 April 1878, Page 4

⁶⁴ Staffordshire Advertiser: 27 April 1878, Page 7

⁶⁵ Walsall Observer and South Staffordshire Chronicle: 3 August 1878, Page 3

⁶⁶ General Register Office. England and Wales Civil Registration Indexes. London, England: Alice REEVES born Walsall Q2/1879 (Volume 6b, Page 758). Mothers name HAWLEY.

⁶⁷ General Register Office. England and Wales Civil Registration Indexes. London, England: Alice REEVES died aged 0 years at Walsall Q3/1879 (Volume 6b, Page 311)

⁶⁸ Walsall Observer and South Staffordshire Chronicle: 23 August 1879, Page 2

⁶⁹ General Register Office. England and Wales Civil Registration Indexes. London, England: Frances REEVES born Walsall Q3/1880 (Volume 6b, Page 667). Mothers name HAWLEY.

⁷⁰ Walsall Observer and South Staffordshire Chronicle: 1 May 1880, Page 3

⁷¹ Lichfield Mercury: 17 September 1880, Page 7

⁷² Walsall Observer and South Staffordshire Chronicle: 18 September 1880. Page 2

⁷³ General Register Office. England and Wales Civil Registration Indexes. London, England: James HAMMONDS married Lucy RUFF at Walsall Q1/1881 (Volume 6b, Page 726)

⁷⁴ Walsall Observer and South Staffordshire Chronicle: 12 February 1881, Page 7

⁷⁵ Walsall Observer and South Staffordshire Chronicle: 26 February 1881, Page 8

⁷⁶ Walsall Observer and South Staffordshire Chronicle: 12 February 1881, Page 7

[77] Census Returns of England and Wales, 1881. Class: RG11; Piece: 2822; Folio: 104; Page: 21; GSU roll: 1341675

[78] Census Returns of England and Wales, 1881. Class: RG11; Piece: 2828; Folio: 16; Page: 25; GSU roll: 1341677

[79] Census Returns of England and Wales, 1881. Class: RG11; Piece: 2824; Folio: 41; Page: 18; GSU roll: 1341676

[80] Census Returns of England and Wales, 1881. Class: RG11; Piece: 2828; Folio: 120; Page: 46; GSU roll: 1341677

[81] Census Returns of England and Wales, 1881. Class: RG11; Piece: 2823; Folio: 76; Page: 26; GSU roll: 1341676

[82] Census Returns of England and Wales, 1881. Class: RG11; Piece: 2828; Folio: 5; Page: 4; GSU roll: 1341677

[83] Census Returns of England and Wales, 1881. Class: RG11; Piece: 2828; Folio: 28; Page: 5; GSU roll: 1341677

[84] General Register Office. England and Wales Civil Registration Indexes. London, England: Emma REEVES aged 30 years died in Walsall Q1/1882 (Volume 6b, Page 422)

[85] General Register Office. England and Wales Civil Registration Indexes. London, England: Edwin HAMMOND married Annie MILNER at Walsall Q2/1882 (Volume 6b, Page 961)

[86] Walsall Observer and South Staffordshire Chronicle: 15 April 1882, Page 8

[87] General Register Office. England and Wales Civil Registration Indexes. London, England: born in Walsall Q3/1878 (Volume 6b, Page 698). No Mothers name.

[88] General Register Office. England and Wales Civil Registration Indexes. London, England: William Edward DOLFIN married Sophia STANGER in Walsall Q3/1880 (Volume 6b, Page 780)

[89] England, Births and Christenings, 1538-1975: FHL Film Number: 1526194 IT 17-19

[90] General Register Office. England and Wales Civil Registration Indexes. London, England: Abel REEVES and Sophia STANGHUD married in Walsall Q1/1883 (Volume 6b, Page 814)

[91] General Register Office. England and Wales Civil Registration Indexes. London, England: William Edward DOLPHIN died aged 38 years in Walsall Q1/1886 (Volume 6b, Page 472)

[92] General Register Office. England and Wales Civil Registration Indexes. London, England: Benjamin HAMMOND married Matilda RUFF at Walsall Q1/1883 (Volume 6b, Page 839)

[93] Walsall Observer and South Staffordshire Chronicle: 3 March 1883, Page 5

[94] Walsall Observer and South Staffordshire Chronicle: 31 March 1883, Page 7

[95] Walsall Observer and South Staffordshire Chronicle: 12 May 1883, Page 5

[96] Birmingham Daily Post: 29 August 1883, Page 8

[97] Birmingham Daily Post: 13 September 1883, Page 8

[98] Walsall Observer and South Staffordshire Chronicle: 29 December 1883, Page 5

[99] General Register Office. England and Wales Civil Registration Indexes. London, England: Rose Lilian REEVES born Walsall Q3/1883 (Volume 6b, Page 687). Mothers name HAWLEY.

[100] Birmingham Daily Post: 30 January 1884, Page 8

[101] Walsall Observer and South Staffordshire Chronicle: 2 February 1884, Page 6

[102] Walsall Observer and South Staffordshire Chronicle: 5 July 1884, Page 7

[103] Birmingham Daily Post: 2 July 1884, Page 8

[104] Staffordshire Advertiser: 16 August 1884

[105] General Register Office. England and Wales Civil Registration Indexes. London, England: Benjamin HAMMOND died aged 29 years at Stafford Q3/1884 (Volume 6b, Page 6)

[106] General Register Office. England and Wales Civil Registration Indexes. London, England: Edward James HAMMOND born Walsall Q2/1885 (Volume 6b, Page 708)

[107] Walsall Observer and South Staffordshire Chronicle: 25 October 1884, Page 8

[108] General Register Office. England and Wales Civil Registration Indexes. London, England: Margaret HAMMOND died aged 64 years at Walsall Q4/1884 (Volume 6b, Page 437)

[109] General Register Office. England and Wales Civil Registration Indexes. London, England: George Thomas REEVES born Walsall Q1/1885 (Volume 6b, Page 775). Mothers name HAWLEY.

[110] Walsall Observer and South Staffordshire Chronicle: 27 March 1886, Page 8

[111] General Register Office. England and Wales Civil Registration Indexes. London, England: George Thomas REEVES died aged 1 year at Walsall Q3/1886 (Volume 6b, Page 382).

[112] General Register Office. England and Wales Civil Registration Indexes. London, England: Laura Louisa REEVES born at Walsall Q4/1886 (Volume 6b, Page 698). Mothers name HAWLEY.

[113] General Register Office. England and Wales Civil Registration Indexes. London, England: Gertrude REEVES born at Walsall Q4/1886 (Volume 6b, Page 698). Mothers name HAWLEY.

[114] General Register Office. England and Wales Civil Registration Indexes. London, England: Gertrude REEVES died aged 0 years at Walsall Q4/1886 (Volume 6b, Page 408).

[115] General Register Office. England and Wales Civil Registration Indexes. London, England: Laura Louisa REEVES died aged 0 years at Walsall Q1/1887 (Volume 6b, Page 439).

[116] Walsall Observer and South Staffordshire Chronicle: 17 July 1886, Page 3

[117] Walsall Observer and South Staffordshire Chronicle: 25 September 1886, Page 7

[118] General Register Office. England and Wales Civil Registration Indexes. London, England: William REEVES died aged 50 Walsall Q4/1887 (Volume 6b, Page 387)

[119] Walsall Observer and South Staffordshire Chronicle: 11 December 1886, Page 7

[120] Walsall Observer and South Staffordshire Chronicle: 7 May 1887, Page 8

[121] Walsall Observer and South Staffordshire Chronicle: 2 July 1887, Page 7

[122] Walsall Observer and South Staffordshire Chronicle: 23 July 1887, Page 8

[123] Walsall Observer and South Staffordshire Chronicle: 13 August 1887, Page 3

[124] Walsall Observer and South Staffordshire Chronicle: 28 January 1888, Page 8

[125] Walsall Observer and South Staffordshire Chronicle: 7 April 1888, Page 8

[126] Walsall Observer and South Staffordshire Chronicle: 5 May 1888, Page 8

[127] Lichfield Mercury: 18 May 1888, Page 3

[128] Walsall Observer and South Staffordshire Chronicle: 2 June 1888, Page 5

[129] Lichfield Mercury: 8 June 1888, Page 6

[130] Walsall Observer and South Staffordshire Chronicle: 9 June 1888, Page 5

[131] General Register Office. England and Wales Civil Registration Indexes. London, England: Enoch Edward REEVES born in Walsall Q4/1888 (Volume 6b, Page 655). Mothers name HAWLEY.

[132] Walsall Observer and South Staffordshire Chronicle: 5 January 1889, Page 7

[133] Walsall Observer and South Staffordshire Chronicle: 26 October 1889, Page 5

[134] Birmingham Daily Post: 21 November 1889, Page 8

[135] General Register Office. England and Wales Civil Registration Indexes. London, England: Benjamin HAMMOND died aged 66 years at Walsall Q4/1889 (Volume 6b, Page 410)

[136] Walsall Observer and South Staffordshire Chronicle: 18 January 1890, Page 7

[137] Birmingham Daily Post: 18 April 1889, Page 7

[138] General Register Office. England and Wales Civil Registration Indexes. London, England: Robert JONES married Matilda HAMMOND at Walsall Q3/1890 (Volume 6b, Page 997)

[139] Walsall Observer and South Staffordshire Chronicle: 15 March 1890, Page 5

[140] General Register Office. England and Wales Civil Registration Indexes. London, England: Arthur Ernest REEVES born Walsall Q2/1890 (Volume 6b, Page 733). Mothers name HAWLEY.

[141] Walsall Observer and South Staffordshire Chronicle: 17 January 1891, Page 6

[142] Birmingham Daily Post: 13 January 1891, Page 7

[143] Walsall Observer and South Staffordshire Chronicle: 24 January 1891, Page 5

[144] Walsall Observer and South Staffordshire Chronicle: 16 May 1891, Page 3

[145] Census Returns of England and Wales, 1891. Class: RG12; Piece: 2255; Folio: 60; Page: 8; GSU roll: 6097365

[146] Census Returns of England and Wales, 1891. Class: RG12; Piece: 2255; Folio: 16; Page: 25; GSU roll: 6097365

[147] Census Returns of England and Wales, 1891. Class: RG12; Piece: 2255; Folio: 18; Page: 30; GSU roll: 6097365

[148] Census Returns of England and Wales, 1891. Class: RG12; Piece: 2249; Folio: 120; Page: 16; GSU roll: 6097359

[149] Census Returns of England and Wales, 1891. Class: RG12; Piece: 2254; Folio: 91; Page: 20; GSU roll: 6097364

[150] Census Returns of England and Wales, 1891. Class: RG12; Piece: 2254; Folio: 90; Page: 18; GSU roll: 6097364

[151] Census Returns of England and Wales, 1891. Class: RG12; Piece: 2254; Folio: 99; Page: 35; GSU roll: 6097364 and Class: RG12; Piece: 2254; Folio: 99; Page: 36; GSU roll: 6097364

[152] Walsall Observer and South Staffordshire Chronicle: 11 July 1891, Page 7

[153] Birmingham Daily Post: 7 July 1891, Page 7

[154] General Register Office. England and Wales Civil Registration Indexes. London, England: David Sidney REEVES born Walsall Q1/1892 (Volume 6b, Page 726). Mothers name HAWLEY.

[155] Walsall Advertiser: 17 June 1893, Page 2

[156] Walsall Advertiser: 19 August 1893, Page 2

[157] Walsall Advertiser: 19 May 1894, Page 2

[158] General Register Office. England and Wales Civil Registration Indexes. London, England: Ada Edith REEVES born Walsall Q1/1894 (Volume 6b, Page 751). Mothers name HAWLEY.

[159] Staffordshire Baptisms: St Paul's, Walsall, Page 208, Affiliate Image Identifier: D3672/1/3

[160] General Register Office. England and Wales Civil Registration Indexes. London, England: Ada Edith REEVES died aged 0 years at Walsall Q1/1894 (Volume 6b, Page 483)

[161] Berrow's Worcester Journal: 22 September 1894, Page 4

[162] Berrow's Worcester Journal: 29 September 1894, Page 5

[163] Berrow's Worcester Journal: 13 October 1894, Page 4

[164] UK, Calendar of Prisoners, 1868-1929: Reference: HO 140/157

[165] Birmingham Daily Post: 16 October 1894, Page 5

[166] England and Wales Civil Registration Indexes. London, England: Annie REEVES born Walsall Q1/1895 (Volume 6b, Page 808). Mothers name HAWLEY.

[167] General Register Office. England and Wales Civil Registration Indexes. London, England: Robert STANTON married Susan Emily THORPE at Walsall Q2/1895 (Volume 6b, Page 1037)

[168] Staffordshire Marriages: St. John's, Walsall, Page 16 Affiliate Image Identifier: D3627/10

[169] Walsall Observer and South Staffordshire Chronicle: 4 July 1896, Page 7

[170] Lichfield Mercury: 17 July 1896, Page 7

[171] Walsall Advertiser: 18 July 1896, Page 6

[172] Staffordshire Advertiser: 4 July 1896, Page 7

[173] General Register Office. England and Wales Civil Registration Indexes. London, England: Sarah REEVES died aged 41 years at Walsall Q1/1899 (Volume 6b, Page 649)

[174] Walsall Observer and South Staffordshire Chronicle: 2 September 1899, Page 5

[175] 1900 United States Federal Census: Year: 1900; Census Place: Salt Lake City Ward 2, Salt Lake, Utah; Page: 11; Enumeration District: 0027; FHL microfilm: 1241684

[176] British Army Service Records 1760-1915: Wo 97 - Chelsea Pensioners British Army Service Records 1760-1913: Box   5757

[177] British Army World War I Pension Records 1914-1920 - WO364: WO364; Piece: 3220

[178] England and Wales Civil Registration Indexes. London, England: Sarah BULLOWS died aged 61 years at Walsall Q3/1900 (Volume 6b, Page 465)

[179] Census Returns of England and Wales, 1901. Kew, Surrey, England: Class: RG13; Piece: 2704; Folio: 68; Page: 5

[180] England and Wales Civil Registration Indexes. London, England: Edward Hammond REEVES born Walsall Q2/1901 (Volume 6b, Page 771)

[181] England and Wales Civil Registration Indexes. London, England: Edward Hammond REEVES died age 0 years at Walsall Q2/1901 (Volume 6b, Page 448)

[182] England and Wales Civil Registration Indexes. London, England: Edward Hammond REEVES born Walsall Q3/1902 (Volume 6b, Page 809)

[183] England and Wales Civil Registration Indexes. London, England: Edward Hammond REEVES died age 0 years at Walsall Q3/1902 (Volume 6b, Page 371)

[184] Census Returns of England and Wales, 1901. Kew, Surrey, England: Class: RG13; Piece: 2701; Folio: 96; Page: 16 & 17

[185] England and Wales Civil Registration Indexes. London, England: Thomas REEVES married Florence WOOTTEN at Walsall Q2/1905 (Volume 6b, Page 1147)

[186] Census Returns of England and Wales, 1901. Kew, Surrey, England: Class: *RG13*; Piece: *2826*; Folio: *48*; Page: *37*

[187] England and Wales Civil Registration Indexes. London, England: Alfred WOOTTEN married Sarah Jane REEVES at Walsall Q4/1897 (Volume 6b, Page 1243)

[188] Census Returns of England and Wales, 1901. Kew, Surrey, England: Class: RG13; Piece: 2826; Folio: 48; Page: 37

[189] Census Returns of England and Wales, 1901. Kew, Surrey, England: Class: RG13; Piece: 2700; Folio: 140; Page: 46 & 47

[190] Census Returns of England and Wales, 1901. Kew, Surrey, England: Class: RG13; Piece: 3304; Folio: 59; Page: 22

[191] England and Wales Civil Registration Indexes. London, England: John Thomas REEVES married Ada Alice THORPE at Walsall Q3/1907 (Volume 6b, Page 1414)

[192] British Army Militia Service Records, 1806-1915 - WO96: Box 667, Record 334

[193] British Army Service Records 1760-1915 - WO97: Box 5757, Record 14

[194] British Army World War I Service Records, 1914-1920 - WO363

[195] British Army Militia Service Records, 1806-1915 - WO96: Box 667 Record 330

[196] Walsall Advertiser: 19 November 1904, Page 5

[197] Walsall Observer and South Staffordshire Chronicle: 30 June 1906, Page 7

[198] Walsall Advertiser: 24 August 1907, Page 7

[199] Lichfield Mercury: 30 April 1909, Page 5

[200] Lichfield Mercury: 28 December 1923, Page 8

[201] Lichfield Mercury: 11 October 1907, Page 8

[202] The Tamworth Herald: 12 October 1907, Page 8

[203] Lichfield Mercury: 18 October 1907, Page 5

[204] Staffordshire Advertiser: 19 October 1907, Page 7

[205] Walsall Advertiser: 19 October 1907, Page 4

[206] The Tamworth Herald: 19 October 1907, Page 7

[207] Lichfield Mercury: 25 October 1907, Page 5

[208] The Tamworth Herald: 26 October 1907, Page 7

[209] Staffordshire Advertiser: 26 October 1907, Page 7

[210] Walsall Advertiser: 26 October 1907, Page 4

[211] Boston, Massachusetts. Passenger Lists of Vessels Arriving at Boston, Massachusetts, 1891-1943: Records of the Immigration and Naturalization Service, 1787-2004; Record Group Number: 85; Series Number: T843; NARA Roll Number: 128

[212] The Boston Globe: 24 January 1909, Page 13

[213] The Philadelphia Inquirer: 25 January 1909, Page 1 & 2

[214] Salt Lake Telegram: 23 July 1909, Page 3

[215] The Inter Mountain Republican: 23 July 1909, Page 8

[216] Utah, U.S., Select County Marriages, 1887-1937: FHL Film Number: 429074

[217] Utah, U.S., Select Marriage Index, 1887-1985: Certificate Number: A010400

[218] Walsall Observer and South Staffordshire Chronicle: 28 May 1910, Page 5

[219] Walsall Advertiser: 28 May 1910, Page 3

[220] Walsall Observer and South Staffordshire Chronicle: 7 January 1911, Page 6

[221] Census Returns of England and Wales, 1911. Kew, Surrey, England: Registration District Number: 370, Sub-registration District: Walsall, ED, institution, or vessel: 21, Piece: 17178.

[222] Census Returns of England and Wales, 1911. Kew, Surrey, England: Registration District Number: 370, Sub-registration District: Walsall, ED, institution, or vessel: 10 Piece: 17167.

[223] Census Returns of England and Wales, 1911. Kew, Surrey, England: Registration District Number: 370, Sub-registration District: Walsall, ED, institution, or vessel: 21 Piece: 17178.

[224] Census Returns of England and Wales, 1911. Kew, Surrey, England: Military Unit: Infantry 1st Bn South Staffordshire Regt, Registration District Number: 641, ED, institution, or vessel: Arabia, Cyprus, and Gibraltar, Piece: 34996.

[225] Census Returns of England and Wales, 1911. Kew, Surrey, England: Registration District Number: 370, Sub-registration District: Walsall, ED, institution, or vessel: 10 Piece: 17167.

[226] Census Returns of England and Wales, 1911. Kew, Surrey, England: Registration District Number: 370, Sub-registration District: Walsall, ED, institution, or vessel: 25 Piece: 17182.

[227] Census Returns of England and Wales, 1911. Kew, Surrey, England: Registration District Number: 370, Sub-registration District: Walsall, ED, institution, or vessel: 11 Piece: 17168.

[228] Census Returns of England and Wales, 1911. Kew, Surrey, England: Registration District Number: 370, Sub-registration District: Walsall, ED, institution, or vessel: 13 Piece: 17170.

[229] Census Returns of England and Wales, 1911. Kew, Surrey, England: Registration District Number: 370, Sub-registration District: Walsall, ED, institution, or vessel: 12 Piece: 17169.

[230] Census Returns of England and Wales, 1911. Kew, Surrey, England: Registration District Number: 370, Sub-registration District: Aldridge, ED, institution, or vessel: 11 Piece: 17198.

[231] England and Wales Civil Registration Indexes. London, England: Eliza Margaret HAMMONDS born Walsall Q3/1983 (Volume 6b, Page 683). Mothers name RUFF.

[232] England and Wales Civil Registration Indexes. London, England: Edward James HAMMOND born Walsall Q2/1885 (Volume 6b, Page 708). Mother name RUFF.

[233] England and Wales Civil Registration Indexes. London, England: Richard Thomas HAMMONDS born Walsall Q3/1889 (Volume 6b, Page 702)

[234] England and Wales Civil Registration Indexes. London, England: Alfred Isaac JONES born Walsall Q2/1893 (Volume 6b, Page 817). Mothers name RUFF.

[235] England and Wales Civil Registration Indexes. London, England: Robert JONES married Matilda HAMMOND at Walsall Q3/1890 (Volume 6b, Page 997)

[236] England and Wales Civil Registration Indexes. London, England: Robert PHILLIPS married Eliza HAMMOND at Walsall Q4/1903 (Volume 6b, Page 1286)

[237] Census Returns of England and Wales, 1911. Kew, Surrey, England: Registration District Number: 370, Sub-registration District: Walsall, ED, institution, or vessel: 13 Piece: 17170.

[238] Walsall Advertiser: 8 July 1911, Page 9

[239] Walsall Advertiser: 1 July 1911, Page 9

[240] Walsall Observer and South Staffordshire Chronicle: 16 September 1911, Page 7

[241] Walsall Advertiser: 20 July 1912, Page 4

[242] Walsall Advertiser: 23 August 1913, Page 3

[243] Salt Lake Herald: 6 January 1913, Page 5

[244] Salt Lake Herald: 8 January 1913, Page 5

[245] Staffordshire Advertiser: 28 February 1914, Page 4

[246] Walsall Advertiser: 14 March 1914, Page 10

[247] Salt Lake Telegram: 15 April 1914, Page 16

[248] Walsall Observer, and South Staffordshire Chronicle: 15 August 1914, Page 3

[249] First World War Representative Medical Records of Servicemen and Servicewomen - MH 106: MH 106/1397

[250] First World War Representative Medical Records of Servicemen and Servicewomen - MH 106: MH106/1407

[251] UK, British Army World War I Medal Rolls Index Cards, 1914-1920: William H. Reeves

[252] Lichfield Mercury: 23 October 1914, Page 5

[253] Walsall Observer and South Staffordshire Chronicle: 24 October 1914, Page 5

254 Walsall Observer and South Staffordshire Chronicle: 31 October 1914, Page 7

255 Walsall Observer and South Staffordshire Chronicle: 28 November 1914, Page 7

256 Walsall Advertiser: 5 December 1914, Page 7

257 England and Wales Civil Registration Indexes. London, England: Arthur E REEVES married Eliza WEBB at Walsall Q3/1915 (Volume 6b, Page 1673)

258 Walsall Observer and South Staffordshire Chronicle: 12 August 1916, Page 5

259 UK, Commonwealth War Graves, 1914-1921 and 1939-1947: THIEPVAL MEMORIAL

260 De Ruvigny's Roll of Honour 1914-24: Volume 2, Page 258

261 British Army World War I Service Records, 1914-1920 - WO363: Army Service Corp - Driver T/20408 John REEVE

262 Unit Register Card: In authors possession

263 Walsall Observer and South Staffordshire Chronicle: 17 March 1917, Page 3

264 British Army World War I Pension Records 1914-1920 - WO364; Piece: 1503

265 First World War Representative Medical Records of Servicemen and Servicewomen - MH 106: MH106/1137

266 Walsall Observer and South Staffordshire Chronicle: 13 October 1917, Page 3

267 UK, Army Registers of Soldiers' Effects, 1901-1929: Record Number Ranges: 580001-581500; Reference: 338

268 Walsall Observer and South Staffordshire Chronicle: 20 October 1917, Page 8

269 Walsall Observer and South Staffordshire Chronicle: 19 August 1916, Page 5

270 British Army World War I Pension Records 1914-1920 - WO364: WO364; Piece: 3919

271 UK, Army Registers of Soldiers' Effects, 1901-1929: NAM Accession Number: 1991-02-333; Record Number Ranges: 821501-823000; Reference: 499

272 UK, Soldiers Died in the Great War, 1914-1919: Rank: Private, Regiment: Lincolnshire Regiment, Battalion: 5th Battalion, Regimental Number: 53224, Type of Casualty: Died of wounds, Theatre of War: Western European Theatre

[273] British Army World War I Pension Records 1914-1920 - WO364: WO364; Piece: 1503

[274] British Army World War I Service Records, 1914-1920 - WO363: Corporal 89168 HAMMOND, Royal Garrison Artillery

[275] London Gazette: 12 March 1918 - Page 3237 Supplement

[276] Utah, U.S., Death and Military Death Certificates, 1904-1961: Series Number: 81448

[277] 1916-09-09 - Deseret Evening News - Page 2: 9 September 1916, Page 2

[278] Salt Lake Tribune: 29 December 1916, Page 5

[279] Deseret Evening News: 14 August 1917, Page 2

[280] U.S., World War I Draft Registration Cards, 1917-1918

[281] California, U.S., Federal Naturalization Records, 1843-1999

[282] England and Wales Civil Registration Indexes. London, England: Enoch Edward REECE married Eliza WEBB at Walsall Q3/1919 (Volume 6b, Page 1840)

[283] California, U.S., Death Index, 1905-1939

[284] Riverbank News: 6 April 1923, Page 3

[285] England and Wales Civil Registration Indexes. London, England: Edward HAMMOND died aged 62 years at Walsall Q2/1924 (Volume 6b, Page 690)

[286] England and Wales Civil Registration Indexes. London, England: Abel REEVES died aged 78 in Walsall Q4/1931 (Volume 6b, Page 705)

[287] California, County Birth and Death Records, 1800-1994

[288] England and Wales Civil Registration Indexes. London, England: Enoch E REEVES aged 48 years died Walsall Q1/1936 (Volume 6b, Page 843)

[289] Utah, County Marriages, 1871-1941

[290] Utah Death Certificates, 1904-1965

[291] England and Wales Civil Registration Indexes. London, England: Frances BLOOD died aged 60 years at Walsall Q3/1939 (Volume 6b, Page 848)

[292] England and Wales Civil Registration Indexes. London, England: Rose L SMITH died aged 47 years at Walsall Q2/1940 (Volume 6b, Page 1305)

[293] England and Wales Civil Registration Indexes. London, England: James HAMMOND died aged 91 years at Walsall Q4/1945 (Volume 6b, Page 641)

[294] England and Wales Civil Registration Indexes. London, England: William H REEVES died aged 68 years at Walsall Q3/1946 (Volume 9b, Page 531)

[295] England and Wales Civil Registration Indexes. London, England: Robert STANTON died aged 74 years at Walsall Q4/1949 (Volume 9b, Page 669)

Printed in Great Britain
by Amazon